The Ultimate Guide to Chinese Tea

The Ultimate Guide to Chinese Tea

Bret Hinsch

White Lotus Press

To Allen

White Lotus Co., Ltd
G.P.O. Box 1141
Bangkok 10501
Thailand

Tel.   (66) 0-38239-883-4
Fax   (66) 0-38239-885
E-mail   ande@loxinfo.co.th
Website   http://thailine.com/lotus

Printed in Thailand

Designed and typeset by COMSET Limited Partnership

ISBN   978-974-480-129-6   pbk.   White Lotus Co., Ltd., Bangkok

Table of Contents

Preface

My decision to write this book was sparked by a conversation I had several years ago at my favorite place in Taipei, an elegant teashop called Wang De Chuan. One of their sales staff at the time was an energetic young tea fanatic who happily chattered away about her favorite subject while brewing samples of the spring harvest. In addition to devouring countless Chinese books and articles on tea, she had also read whatever she could find on the subject in English and in Japanese. In Taiwan, buying tea is never rushed, and a purchase involves plenty of tasting and leisurely conversation. As we sipped green tea and chatted, she lamented that everything she had read in English about Chinese tea was riddled with errors. Shaking her head with heartfelt sympathy for all the benighted foreigners denied reliable information about her passion, she asked why English writing about Chinese tea was so pitiful. Not only did I heartily agree with her complaint, but I also decided to do something about it.

I feel fortunate to have lived in Taiwan for the past fifteen years. This lush sub-tropical island not only has some of the world's top tea fields but also boasts a sophisticated culture of connoisseurship. Visiting the superb local teahouses and teashops has allowed me to taste representative teas from across China. And because I speak and read Chinese, I have also been able to consult Chinese books and articles for technical information about tea growing, harvesting, processing, and drinking. I have done my best to make this book accurate and reliable, searching out representative teas to taste, reading extensively, talking with local experts, attending professional tea-tastings, and consulting multiple Chinese sources to crosscheck key facts.

Despite my determination to approach the subject with rigor, not everything here comes from personal observation. China is an enormous country, and I have not visited all the major tea-growing regions. I was unable to acquire some teas that are mostly consumed locally, so at times I have had to rely upon second-hand descriptions. Also, I am neither a tea-grower nor tea-processor, but merely an enthusiastic drinker, so none of the technical information given here comes from my personal experience. Despite these compromises, I have done everything I could to ensure that this book is accurate and comprehensive.

My most important insights came from years of tasting experience as well as many hours of leisurely conversation in teashops and teahouses. I should like to thank the staff of Wang De Chuan in particular. They carry the finest line of teas I have ever encountered, and their knowledgeable staff members have been able to answer every question I have ever put to them. Geow Yong Tea Hong teashop, also in Taipei, carries a superb selection of Wuyi oolongs, and they were delighted to help me navigate the bewildering range of teas from that remarkable mountain. I was shown great kindness by everyone at the *Puer* Tea Museum in Yingge, Taiwan, and they spent considerable time patiently explaining the ins and outs of *puer* tea. They also allowed me to taste different kinds of rare *puer* from their extensive collection, including some very old and expensive teas, to illustrate some of the finer points of *puer* connoisseurship. I have also spent considerable time at many other teashops in Taipei and Hong Kong, too numerous to mention, gleaning useful information wherever I went.

In addition, I learned quite a bit from frequenting teahouses in Taipei and the surrounding tea country. Among these, the staff of Wisteria proved especially knowledgeable, and their wide selection of teas and periodic tasting events gave me the chance to experience certain obscure brews. I should also like to thank my friends and colleagues who remembered me while traveling through China and brought back unusual regional teas for me to taste. Their generosity and thoughtfulness broadened my tasting experience considerably.

For information about tea history and processing, I have had to rely upon publications in Chinese. The best source for researching Chinese tea is the behemoth encyclopedia *Zhongguo chajing* [*Classic of Chinese Tea*], edited by Chen Zongmao. Most of my technical information concerning harvesting and processing was gleaned from that massive work. Jing Hong's *Mingcha zhanggu* [*Grasping the Past of Famous Teas*] and some other works provided alternate sources for checking basic facts. *Zhongguo cha, Taiwan cha* [*Chinese Tea/ Taiwanese Tea*], written in Japanese by Kaori Arimoto and subsequently translated into Chinese, provides concise and useful background information on many famous teas. Chi Zongxian's *Zoujin Zhongguocha de shijie* [*Entering the World of Chinese Tea*] is a trove of invaluable information. Two more books by Chi Zongxian, *Wuyi cha* [*Wuyi Tea*] and *Hangzhou Longjing*, demystified those confusing subjects. *Taibei zhao cha* [*Taipei Tea Talk*] by Wu Deliang is an excellent introduction to the oolongs of northern Taiwan. And Gong Zhi's *Zhongguo gongcha* [*Chinese Tribute Tea*] introduces the history of elite tea-drinking customs. In addition, I sought out specialized collections of historical documents and classic books on tea for more detailed information about tea history.

I learned a great deal about the daunting subject of *puer* from the superb book *Dangdai puer cha* [*Contemporary* Puer *Tea*] by Huang Jianliang and Cong Jianxing. In addition, *Puer cha* [Puer *Tea*] by Zhou Hongjie contains detailed technical information on the chemistry and biology of tea, oxidation, and the ageing process. I also went through back issues of the Taiwanese magazine *Puer cha* [Puer *Tea*], which provided highly detailed technical information about *puer* and other kinds of tea. In addition to these major sources, I also consulted a number of other Chinese books and articles for information about specific points.

Chinese Pronunciation

Although there are several ways to write the sounds of Mandarin Chinese with roman letters, the *pinyin* system is now the standard one. Westerners find Mandarin notoriously difficult to pronounce, so it should not be a surprised if native speakers are unable to understand what you are attempting to say.

The below chart gives some rough English equivalents to *pinyin*. Unless otherwise indicated, the pronunciation of a letter is similar to English. A glossary with *pinyin* and Chinese characters is included at the end of this book. Pointing to the Chinese characters in question will guarantee that a native speaker will understand the word intended.

Pinyin	**English Equivalent**
a	ah
e	uh
i (after h)	ur (as in "fur")
i (after s, c, z)	i (as in "lift")
i (elsewhere)	ee (as in "sheet")
ian or yan	yen
ui	way
u (after q, j, x, or y)	French *u* or German *ü*
u (elsewhere)	oo (as in "food")
ü	French *u* or German *ü*
yu	French *u* or German *ü*

c	ts (as in hats)
ch	ch (as in church)
chi	chur (as in churn; the "i" is silent)
ci	ts + i (as in "lift")
g	hard g (as in "go")
j	j (as in "John," not like the "g" in "beige")
q	ch (as in "church")
r- (initial)	between American "r" and the French initial j
-r (final)	r
ri	French j followed by an American "r" (the "i" is silent)
s	s (as in "snake")
sh	sh (as in "shoot")
shi	shir (as in "shirt"; the "i" is silent)
si	sz + i (as in "lift")
x	sh (as in "shoot")
z	ds (as in "heads")
zh	j (as in "John," not like the French j)
zhi	jer (as in "jersey")
zi	dz + i (as in "lift")

Chronology of Chinese Dynasties

(All dates as per Common Era)

25–220	Eastern Han
618–907	Tang
960–1279	Song
1279–1368	Yuan
1368–1644	Ming
1644–1911	Qing

Part I

Getting Started

Chapter 1

The Basics

Imagine a drink that sometimes tastes like vanilla but can also taste like curry. And seaweed. And plum. Not to mention mushroom, egg yolk, camphor, grass, tangerine, and chocolate. The teas of China encompass all of these flavors and infinitely more. Chinese tea is quite simply the world's most delicious, healthiest, and most varied beverage. As you begin to explore this sublime drink, you enter a profoundly cultured world filled with intense sensory pleasures and enlivened by the wisdom of an ancient civilization.

Unfortunately, fine tea sometimes resists easy appreciation. The names of Chinese teas are difficult to remember or even pronounce. And although the plethora of teas presents almost limitless variety, this vast array of choices can seem daunting to the uninitiated. Then again, instead of seeing the huge number of unfamiliar teas as an impediment, you should view it as an opportunity. Tea appreciation would not be nearly so much fun if it were not so complex. As you begin to investigate the subject, this strange new world will quickly start to look familiar, and before you know it you will be an old Chinese tea hand.

When it comes to tea, knowledge is power. For centuries, tea-drinkers in the West have been punished for their ignorance. Because few people outside China know the difference between *longjing* and *puer*, the Chinese usually keep the best tea for themselves and pawn off second-rate dross on undiscerning foreign markets. My first contact with Chinese tea consisted of buying some of the gaudy tins of broken leaves that line Chinatown shelves, and quaffing the harsh swill lurking in the stainless steel teapot of the local Cantonese greasy spoon. Only after moving to Asia did I realize that this rubbish is a pale specter of what China's fields have to offer. Once I became determined to teach myself the ins and outs of good tea, I spent many enjoyable hours happily remedying my ignorance. As I gained knowledge and confidence, the pleasures of my tea-drinking hobby steadily increased. By taking the time to educate yourself about tea, you will be able to seek out and appreciate the very best, and I guarantee you will be rewarded with mounting enjoyment.

In a world where so many food products have been homogenized into bland sterility, tea offers the endless stimulation of infinite variety, constantly teasing drinkers with the possibility of serendipitously discovering fascinating new tastes and aromas. Unlike South Asia, where large plantations are the norm, Chinese tea is still mostly a small-scale village handicraft, picked leaf by leaf and heated in small batches over a charcoal fire. During the tea harvest, the mountainsides are covered with farmers carefully selecting and pinching off tea leaves, which they place into large baskets strapped onto their backs, while back home the whole family vigilantly tends piles of oxidizing leaves and periodically heats them with charcoal in fiery woks and smoky brick ovens. Few foods are so labor-intensive. Chinese artisans still make tea by hand, the way all food used to be made. At a time when Americans and Europeans are struggling to preserve pre-industrial food-making traditions, the art of handmade tea is alive and well.

Chinese tea displays the fascinating idiosyncrasies found in any handcrafted product. In each cup of tea you can taste a farmer's unique achievements, making it a profoundly humane beverage. For example, a farmer on the hill behind my home has two fields side by side where he produces the best oolong in the area. The tea from one field has a strong orchid scent; the other carries an intense lemon flavor. His ingenuity in coaxing completely different tastes and aromas from neighboring plants exemplifies the tea farmer's art. The inimitable flavor of his oolong is a personal hallmark, and he takes enormous pride in the fact that his tea is unique. Compare this old-fashioned artistry with the industrial output of the multi-national corporations that control most of our food supply, valuing standardization above all else. Chinese tea is one of the world's last remaining major artisanal food products, and we should all treasure it as a precious remnant of a simpler, more natural way of life.

Unfortunately, obtaining premium tea outside of China is not always easy. As long as foreign consumers remain unaware of the differences between green and oolong tea, cannot tell good from bad, and do not even know how to drink it properly, merchants have no incentive to offer them quality merchandise. And as long as people do not understand what they are buying, of course they will be reluctant or unwilling to spend the money necessary to purchase premium leaves, further discouraging the sale of fine Chinese tea abroad. In other words, this is a chicken-and-egg problem. People cannot appreciate good tea until they have tasted it, but they will not have many chances to taste it until there is a knowledgeable market of educated consumers outside China who appreciate it.

The status of Chinese tea in the West resembles the wine world in the 1950s. Tea and wine are comparable in many ways, and any visitor to a Chinese teashop is immediately reminded of the vocabulary and tasting rituals of wine. However, until the 1960s, most people who lived outside of major grape-growing regions regarded wine appreciation as snobbish and mysterious. Hugh Johnson's landmark 1966 book *Wine* sparked a revolution by offering his readers clear, practical advice. Once consumers learned the basic facts about wine, they bought it with enthusiasm and confidence. The wine marketplace rapidly expanded in scope and sophistication, and good wines are now available at a wide range of prices. Today wine is no longer considered a rarified drink, and people throughout the world see it as a necessary component of the good life.

This book is a manifesto on behalf of Chinese tea, and I hope it can have an impact similar to Johnson's influential work. If we can encourage informed appreciation of Chinese tea outside its ancestral homeland, tea could achieve the status now held by wine. Regardless of how this book is received, I am optimistic that eventually Chinese tea will gain as much recognition and enthusiasm as wine currently enjoys. The dragon is waking up, and people around the world will be affected by the rise of China. Increasing prosperity has already transformed the nation's domestic tea market. The new middle class provides a growing number of educated and demanding consumers. Every year more premium tea is being grown to satisfy the booming domestic market, so now there is now more good tea available than ever before. Moreover, as China resumes its traditional place as a world economic leader, the sophisticated culture of that ancient nation will undoubtedly draw increased attention from people around the world. Not long ago, Americans considered sushi weird and exotic, but now it's a standard offering at supermarkets and malls. Asia has already transformed the way we eat; it is only a matter of time before it also changes the way we drink.

Tea offers all the advantages of wine without its main drawback. Wine buffs almost never mention the chief attraction of fermented grapes: wine is an extremely powerful drug. The moment you begin sipping a glass of wine, gentle inebriation commences and your ability to concentrate on what you are drinking is instantly impaired. If wine did not contain alcohol, would people really drink it simply for the taste? Would connoisseurs build expensive cellars to hold thousands of bottles of interestingly flavored grape juice? Probably not. In contrast, China's sophisticated tea culture is based solely on the appreciation of flavor and aroma. A line by the eighth-century poet Jiao Ran sums up the difference. "The vulgar get drunk on wine, but who can appreciate the benefits of tea's aroma?" For more than fifteen centuries, the subtle flavor of tea has constantly engaged the attention of that nation's greatest minds and palates. Its complex and varied tastes have earned it acclaim since antiquity, despite the absence of mind-numbing alcohol. In fact, the mildly stimulating caffeine in tea actually enhances sensory awareness and helps the appreciation of what is being drunk.

No one questions the health benefits of tea-drinking. Traditional Chinese medicine strongly recommends tea as a general tonic, and a stream of modern scientific research has verified that tea helps prevent many ailments from rheumatoid arthritis to infection. Like fruits and vegetables, tea is rich in antioxidants, chemicals that attack the free radicals responsible for ageing. Antioxidants have also been shown to keep the immune system healthy, reduce the risk of eye diseases, prevent the decline of the brain and nervous system with age, and check the damage to DNA that causes cancer. In addition, antioxidants boost "good cholesterol" (HDL), decrease "bad cholesterol" (LDL), and promote overall cardiovascular health, even if the diet is one high in saturated fats. Unoxidized green tea is higher in antioxidants than the more processed red and black tea, making Chinese tea a healthier choice than the English tea that most people in Western countries currently drink.

As if these miraculous properties were not enough, tea is also extremely nutritious. It contains vital nutrients such as zinc, manganese, potassium, folic acid, and vitamins. Few people know that tea contains fluoride that kills bacteria in the mouth, making it the ideal beverage for dental health. The tea leaf is naturally rich in tannins, a healthy ingredient that already has people flocking to drink red wine. And if you are phobic about caffeine, you will be happy to learn that tea has less than half the caffeine of coffee. Despite being packed full of nutrition, beneficial compounds, and great taste, a cup of tea has no calories, so it's one of those rare miracle foods that can be indulged in as much as one wants.

Even though numerous scientific studies provide objective proof of tea's abundant benefits, you don't need a PhD in biochemistry to know that tea is healthy. Our bodies instinctively recognize that tea is a wholesome beverage. After all, anyone down with the flu will feel a little better after drinking a cup of tea. In an age when so many people poison their systems with chemical soft drinks laced with artificial sweeteners, colorings, and flavorings, it is just commonsense that a purely natural drink is a healthy alternative. Tea-drinkers are people who respect their bodies.

Tea is also extremely flexible. Unlike alcohol, it can be drunk all day long. Not many people would want cola or merlot with breakfast, but a cup of tea is a healthy way to start the day. It goes well with lunch or dinner and is perfect on its own. It is hard to find a wine that goes with curry or chocolate, but the gentle digestive properties of tea make it the perfect accompaniment for spicy, oily, or sweet foods. Even late at night, sun-dried white tea is light enough in caffeine to be a relaxing tisane before bedtime. Most Chinese sip tea between meals as a healthy and natural alternative to soft drinks and alcohol, and health-conscious people everywhere would do well to emulate this habit. Tea is also inexpensive. A pound of leaves is enough to brew hundreds of cups. You might get sticker shock when you look at the price of premium tea leaves, but because you need so little for each pot, fine tea costs much less than wine, coffee, or even soft drinks.

Chinese consider tea-drinking a social occasion. Since tea has an inexplicable power to draw people together, it's the perfect remedy for the isolation and alienation of modern life. A big suburban house surrounded by a lawn might be a symbol of success, but people today often find themselves cut off from the rest of humanity. Tea helps us reconnect with the human race. For some mysterious reason, we are inexorably attracted to the sight of someone drinking tea. A warm teapot magically draws people toward it.

A homey vignette that I have witnessed countless times illustrates tea's magnetic attraction. Almost every day I take a shortcut through a twisty little alley in suburban Taipei. A poor family there keeps their front door open, so over the years I've gotten to observe quite a bit of their daily routine. Although they live in a rundown apartment sparsely furnished with discarded furniture, they nevertheless have an impressive social calendar that would make a grand society doyenne jealous. Whenever I pass by their doorway, I see a group of friends and relatives squeezed around a sagging table to drink tea as they chat, laugh, and nibble toasted melon seeds, the cheapest Taiwanese tea snack. That family might be poor in possessions, but because of their generosity with a teapot, they are always rich in companionship.

The basic definition of good tea is very simple: it should be memorable. If you are still thinking about a cup of tea after you have finished drinking it, it was probably pretty good. Beyond this basic dictum, appreciating tea quickly becomes much more complicated. I have designed this book to introduce the essentials of the subject, giving all of the information you need to start exploring the world of Chinese tea on your own. This chapter provides a general introduction to the basic facts about tea. In the next chapter I give a short history of the drink in its homeland so you can understand how tea evolved and appreciate the exalted place it holds in Chinese culture. Then I discuss the correct way to drink Chinese tea. Most Westerners brew lousy leaves in an oversized pot using water heated to the wrong temperature. No wonder they're often disappointed with the results! Next, I introduce the concepts and vocabulary of Chinese tea connoisseurship, which will make it clear why some teas taste better than others. The bulk of the book is devoted to introducing the finest and most famous examples of the six major types of Chinese tea: white, green, yellow, oolong, red, and black. After reading this book, you will have all the knowledge necessary to buy, prepare, and appreciate good Chinese tea intelligently.

Although tisanes made from various herbs and spices are often called tea, true tea is the leaf of an evergreen tree known to science as *Camellia sinensis*. As the Latin name implies, the tea tree is related to the garden camellia, and it is easy to mistake the two plants at a distance. Some teahouses even keep some potted camellias around to evoke the atmosphere of a tea field. Unlike the ornamental camellia, however, the small white blossoms of the tea tree do not put on much of a show. Under cultivation, tea is usually pruned back to keep it waist high. Clipped tea trees are often grown in low hedges, so most people assume that tea is a bush. In the wild, however, old tea trees are enormous. In their native habitat they can grow to be thirty yards tall with a trunk five feet in circumference. The trademark flavor of tea comes from a considerable amount of natural sugar together with bitter phenolic compounds that evolved as a defense mechanism intended to make these sweet leaves unpalatable to animals. It is this fortuitous interplay between bitter and sweet that makes tea the world's most sublime drink.

Since 1958 botanists have distinguished two major varieties of tea tree, referred to as var. *sinensis* (Chinese tea) and var. *assamica* (Indian tea). The leaves of both types are about the same width, but the *sinensis* leaf is only half as long as the *assamica* leaf, which can reach 6 inches in length. The coarser Indian *assamica* is higher in caffeine and phenolic compounds, and thus has a stronger flavor. For this reason, *assamica* is only suitable for making fully oxidized strong dark tea. Whereas *assamica* makes mediocre green tea, the smaller, more delicate Chinese leaf is well suited to making a whole range of teas from green to red. Some wild tea trees in China's Yunnan Province, close to the native range of the tea tree, have leaves that are much larger than *sinensis*, and these carry assertive flavors. The unusual *assamica*-like leaves grown in Yunnan are put to good use in making hearty aged *puer* black tea. Otherwise, Chinese teas are usually made from the *sinensis* plant. The tea tree is easily hybridized, which accounts for the numerous kinds of tea and the wide area of cultivation. Some hybrids occurred naturally as a result

Old Wild Tea Tree

of random mutations while others were painstakingly developed by innovative tea farmers and more recently by scientists.

Chinese always harvest tea by hand. As with any tree, the leaves closest to the tip of the twig are smallest and youngest. The farmer pinches off a sprout and up to four mature leaves from each twig. Any leaves older than the fourth leaf are too hard and waxy to produce decent tea. The particular combination of sprout and leaves has a major impact on the taste and quality. The sprout is extremely small and grows at the tip of the twig. It is usually folded into the first leaf, which is also quite small. The very finest teas are sometimes made from just the sprout or else the sprout and first leaf. However, each tree produces very few of these, so any tea made from just the small leaves at the tip is inevitably a premium variety. For example, 1 pound of top grade *longjing* tea, made entirely from leaf buds, contains 32–36,000 of these handpicked small leaves. Not surprisingly, good *longjing* is extremely expensive. Most teas consist primarily of the second and third leaves, which are larger and fully opened. The fourth leaf is also sometimes used, usually for low-grade tea. Because the flavor of the leaves tends to decline as one moves down from the tip of the twig, it is useful to examine them before and after brewing to know which leaves you are using. With some experience, you can often determine the type of leaf just by glancing at their shape.

Chinese categorize these leaves by number, a clear-cut and undemanding system. Going down the twig from newest to oldest growths, these are called the sprout, then the first, second, third, and fourth leaves. In the world of Indian tea, however, these leaves have names instead of numbers. Because Western merchants sometimes apply these arcane terms to Chinese teas, it is useful to know what they mean. Indian tea made only from the sprout is called flowery orange pekoe. First leaf tea is orange pekoe, the second leaf is pekoe, the third is pure *souchong*, and the fourth is *souchong*. The word "pekoe" is a bastardization of the Chinese *baihao*, which refers to small furry sprouts, while *souchong* comes from *xiaozhong* meaning "small package" or "small type." Even though these words came from Chinese, they have taken on completely different meanings in English tea jargon.

Each tea harvest is called a flush, the time of year when tea-pickers strap a basket on their backs and make their way down the rows of tea, painstakingly selecting and pinching off the proper combination of leaves from each twig. Some teas have just one flush per year; others have several. The spring flush is usually the best by far. The term tippy, often seen in Western writings about tea, properly refers to second flush Assam tea. After oxidation, these prized Assam leaves are gold rather than black and produce a superior brew. Tippy is also used as a more generic term to

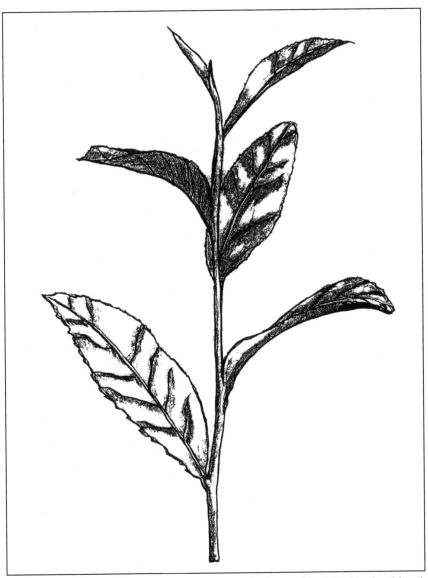

The leaves of the tea tree are called (from top): first leaf, second leaf, third leaf and fourth leaf. The fifth and sixth leaves have a very coarse taste and are usually not harvested.

describe tea made from buds or young leaves, which is what Western merchants mean when they describe a Chinese tea as "tippy." In fact, the well-known Chinese tea varieties usually include some young leaves, so decent Chinese tea is almost always tippy.

The moment a tea leaf is picked, its interior cells begin to break down and oxidation commences. The liquid inside the leaf contains complex enzymes that trigger dramatic chemical transformations when exposed to oxygen. As the enzyme molecules bond with oxygen and create new chemicals, the leaf changes enormously. Large molecules break down, releasing intense aromas, while smaller molecules bond together, modifying the tea's general characteristics. Over time the leaf becomes dark green, then brown, and finally black. As new chemical compounds develop, the aroma changes progressively as well. Oxidation gradually builds molecules so large that they interfere with the natural movement of the surrounding water, giving the liquid a sense of richness.

Most people refer to the oxidation of tea as fermentation, but this is a misnomer. True fermentation usually refers to the action of yeast or bacteria. In contrast, the oxidation of tea takes place through a natural chemical reaction without the help of micro-organisms. When tea is processed, the rate and degree of oxidation are carefully controlled to give the finished product particular characteristics. Oxidation stops when the leaves become either too hot or too dry, which is why processing finishes up with a final heating of the leaves. The degree of oxidation is the most important factor used to classify tea. Contrary to myth, all teas (with the exception of sun-dried white tea) have about the same amount of caffeine, regardless of the degree of oxidation.

Outside of China, tea is usually crudely divided into just two general catchall types: green and black. In the West, green vaguely refers to any tea not fully oxidized. In contrast, Chinese subdivide these "green" teas into much more specific and informative categories: white, green, yellow, and oolong. As for black tea, in the West this term refers to fully oxidized leaves that Chinese call "red tea." To Chinese, however, black tea is a fully oxidized (red) tea that has been fermented through ageing, such as Yunnan *puer* tea. In other words, the Chinese and Western concepts of black tea are entirely different.

The Chinese method for classifying tea is much more precise and informative than the blunt Western distinction between green and black. This sophisticated system divides tea into six general categories based by and large on the degree of oxidation. These are (from lightest to heaviest) white, green, yellow, oolong, red, and black. The first thing an informed Chinese drinker does when presented with an unfamiliar tea is to assign it to one of these six classes. Once you start thinking about tea this way, then instead of being perplexed by thousands of unfamiliar names you will be dealing with just six general kinds of tea. Understanding the common characteristics of each type reveals the underlying order beneath the surface chaos.

White Tea

This is the lightest of all teas. Not only is white tea completely unoxidized, but it usually also has not even been artificially heated. The processing method is the simplest of all. As soon as the leaves are picked, they are laid out in the sun to dry. When sunlight has baked all of the moisture out of the leaves, they are ready for sale. White tea is always dried immediately after harvesting to prevent any oxidation. It is the lightest of all teas, and good white tea has an ineffably delicate aroma and flavor. The leaves produce a very pale liquid with almost no color at all. White tea is relatively low in caffeine, so it is a good choice for the evening. Drink it in a covered cup.

Green Tea

This is the most popular tea in China, and hundreds of varieties are available. Green refers to unoxidized tea artificially heated during processing. The leaves are usually medium- to dark-green, and the liquid ranges in color across shades of yellow and light green. The processing of green tea is fairly simple. Soon after harvesting, the leaves are heated over a fire two or more times to evaporate all of the internal moisture before oxidation has had a chance to begin. Some green teas are rolled to twist them while they are still moist, releasing more flavor onto the surface of the leaf, while the leaves of other teas are carefully flattened so that they end up perfectly straight when dry. Green tea is also produced in Japan, but because Japanese tea is steamed, the flavor is entirely different. Chinese green tea usually has a very light flavor and preserves much of the natural vegetable character of the leaf. Drink it in a covered cup, not a teapot.

Yellow Tea

Yellow tea has been allowed to oxidize very slightly, giving it a fuller flavor than green tea. Nevertheless, yellow tea is still very light and delicate. It can be brewed in either a covered cup or a small teapot. The liquid is light yellow, hence its name. Processing is more complex than green tea. First the leaves are heated in a wok, then they are allowed to oxidize very slightly before being rolled to twist them. The leaves are heated and oxidized either once or repeatedly, depending upon the variety, gradually drying them out. Finally they are heated in an oven to stop oxidization and desiccate them completely. Although most yellow tea undergoes three rounds of oxidation, these are all quite short so the taste is still close to green tea.

Oolong Tea

This term refers to any semi-oxidized tea. Because oolongs occupy the vast middle ground between unoxidized (green) and fully oxidized (red) tea, they are extremely diverse. The color of the liquid ranges from yellow to brown. On one end of the spectrum, Taiwanese oolongs are delicate, sweet, and light, while the more highly oxidized oolongs of Fujian are relatively dark and heavy. Many people refer to this class of tea more generally as semi-oxidized tea. Since every other type of tea has been assigned a color, oolong is sometimes called *qing* tea. *Qing* is a unique Chinese chromatic concept that refers to either green or blue depending upon the context. Because English lacks this mysterious color, I prefer the more traditional name oolong. Processing methods vary considerably. To begin with, the leaves are usually heated over a wok. Then they are either twisted or rolled into balls by hand, and undergo one or more periods of oxidation. Finally, they are dried in an oven to stop oxidation at the right point. Oolong tea is best brewed in a small teapot.

Red Tea

This is the Chinese tea most familiar to Western drinkers, who usually call it black or English tea. During processing, the leaves are allowed to sit until the interior enzymes have oxidized completely. This process turns the leaves dark red or jet black, and they produce the rich red liquid that accounts for the Chinese name. Full oxidation gets rid of much of the natural vegetable flavor of the leaf, but it also removes unpleasant trace flavors as well, so good leaves yield an exceptionally smooth beverage. During processing, the leaves are heated in a wok then usually rolled to twist them. They are allowed to sit until fully oxidized and finally dried out completely in an oven. Good red tea tastes best when brewed in a small teapot, but it can also be prepared in a large pot if preferred.

Black Tea

This term is different from the Western concept of black tea, which the Chinese call red. To Chinese, black refers to red tea that has been allowed to ferment through ageing after processing is complete. The action of microbes, fungi, bacteria, and yeast on the finished tea leaves changes their characteristics considerably. When done correctly, ageing makes red tea very smooth and complex. Any tea can be aged, but only old red tea can be called black. The most famous black tea is *puer* from Yunnan. Black tea is often compressed into bricks or disks, although it also comes in loose-leaf form. Processing methods vary greatly and usually involve initial heating in a wok, rolling to twist the leaves, one or more periods of oxidation, steaming, compression, and drying. Good black tea tastes best in a small teapot, but the flavor is intense enough to hold up to a large pot, which is how the Cantonese usually drink it.

Thinking about the thousands of kinds of tea in terms of these six standard categories simplifies matters considerably. An even simpler system divides Chinese teas into just three types depending upon the degree of oxidation: unoxidized (white and green), semi-oxidized (yellow and oolong), and fully oxidized (red and black). Of course, no matter which classification scheme you prefer, these are only general guidelines. Each tea is grown and processed in a unique way, so even closely related teas have subtle differences. There are innumerable tea tree hybrids, and each produces leaves with different characteristics. Farmers also deliberately tweak many factors in the field to give their tea distinctive flavors and aromas. Different processing methods account for even larger variations. For example, sun-dried teas taste very different from those that have been heated. The degree of oxidation can be varied through an almost infinite number of shades, each of which has a slightly different taste. And baking, roasting in a wok, steaming, and mechanical processing all leave telltale traces.

Tea leaves are sometimes adulterated with flowers or other dried plants to boost their aroma or flavor. In the Tang dynasty, when tea-drinking first became a mainstream custom, it was standard practice to add some dried flowers or other fragrant ingredients, although today most people prefer their tea straight. Most often, middlemen mix in some dried flowers or other fragrant substances to cover up the shortcomings of inferior leaves, so average jasmine tea is usually mediocre. Because floral blends typically use undistinguished leaves, connoisseurs tend to look down on adulterated teas as substandard. To be fair, however, this is not always the case. Some floral mixtures are made with very fine tea, and if done well the result can be very fragrant and delicious. Buying from a shop that deals in high-end teas is the best way to get a decent blend.

Jasmine is the most common flower used to scent tea, and this richly perfumed blend is especially popular in north China. Modern style jasmine tea has been around since the late Ming dynasty. The smell of jasmine is so powerful that it endures long after the petals have been removed from the leaves, so premium jasmine scented tea usually lacks any flowers. In addition to this potent sweet scent, however, jasmine also adds a slightly acrid taste to tea which can be very unpleasant if it is too strong. Tiny dried *osmanthus* flowers, often incorrectly referred to in English as cassia, are another common additive to green and oolong teas. The sweet aroma is very heady, and, if used sparingly, the flavor is not offensive. The scent of dried chrysanthemums is very subdued, and it is a common addition to *puer* tea. If old tea has not been aged properly, dried chrysanthemums help muffle any offensive mildew flavor, so waiters in cheap Cantonese restaurants often throw some chrysanthemums into the pot to camouflage miserable tea. These flowers have a legitimate use as well, however. If aged *puer* is too powerful for your taste, some dried chrysanthemums will tone it down.

In addition to these common flowers, I have also come across dried wild tea tree blossoms. When steeped in hot water, these flowers exude a completely unexpected flavor suggestive of weak smoked tea. The liquid also seems to be extremely high in caffeine. If you can obtain some of these unusual dried flowers, they make a useful booster for anemic tea. Dried tea flowers must be stored in a very dry place, as the slightest amount of damp will make them go bad.

In addition to traditional floral blends, in recent years some middlemen have begun mixing tea with rose petals. This flower has a pleasant scent that goes especially well with oolong. However, you should be extremely careful when buying rose tea. Farmers usually drench roses with pesticides to keep the petals looking pristine. If the roses were not washed prior to drying, you might end up ingesting beautiful poison. To be on the safe side, I suggest buying organic dried rose petals and blending them with the tea leaves yourself.

Dried fruits, essential oils, and medicinal herbs are sometimes added to tea as well. Red tea scented with *litchi* (lychee) is a common export, although this is usually the fate of second-rate leaves. No one would ever want to mask the flavor of fine red tea with overpowering essential oil. Tiny pieces of dried longan (dragon eye), a petite tropical fruit related to the *litchi*, add a rich pleasant flavor to red tea. Longan tea is especially satisfying on a cold winter day. Chinese also sometimes add ginseng to tea. This medicinal herb has a strong earthy flavor and is best avoided unless you believe that ginseng is good for you. (The health value of ginseng has yet to be scientifically proven.)

In addition to these commercial blends, Chinese drinkers sometimes make their own medicinal tea by mixing in dried fruits, berries, flowers, nuts, and various herbs and spices. These pretty mixtures are said to be extremely healthy, and they can have an agreeable flavor, but the tea usually ends up completely hidden beneath all of the other tastes. If you want to try this sort of concoction for yourself you can mix together some dried wolfberries (*gouji*), dried red jujubes, dried chrysanthemum blossoms, dried jasmine blossoms (a tiny amount—just two or three flowers), thinly slivered tangerine peel (fresh or dried), *pang dahai* (*Sterculia scaphigera*, a seed used in Chinese herbal medicine), green tea, and rock sugar. Although some of these ingredients sound formidably exotic, all are readily available in any well-stocked Chinatown grocery store. Just omit the *pang dahai* if you cannot find it. If you brew this medicinal tea in a cup, you can appreciate the attractive mix of colors.

Organic tea is a trend to watch. Until the 1950s, almost all Chinese tea was organic. Farmers were too poor to afford chemical fertilizers and pesticides, so they enriched their soil in the traditional manner with manure, compost, and ashes. Economic development has made agricultural chemicals ubiquitous and now very little organic tea is grown. A few teas are still organic simply because farmers have found it convenient to keep using traditional techniques. Some big leaf tea from Yunnan comes from feral trees, while a small number of lucky farmers living near unruly rivers have their fields naturally fertilized with rich silt during annual floods.

In addition to these traditional natural teas, a small number of farmers have started growing tea using new organic methods. These pioneers face formidable challenges, as the horde of insects native to subtropical regions inevitably ravage tea leaves in the absence of pesticides. Realistically speaking, organic tea is more ideal than reality. China's mammoth cities have some of the world's worst air pollution, and chemical-laden smog inevitably drifts into even the most remote mountain regions where it settles on tea trees. Also, water quality in China is often substandard, and many farmers have no choice but to use polluted water on their crops. Because each tea field is usually quite small, chemical spillover from neighboring plots is difficult to control. So even if a farmer rigorously adheres to organic standards, his trees will nonetheless inevitably absorb some artificial chemicals from the general environment.

Despite this inescapable contamination, a few farmers still strive to produce tea that is as pure and natural as possible, although of course the consumer has to pay a high premium for the extra effort. I wish I could say that organic tea tastes better than its conventional counterparts, but I am afraid that the opposite is usually the case. According to my tasting experience, the flavor and aroma of organic tea is usually quite insipid. Even the organic farmers I have talked to admit that their tea does not taste as good as the conventional product. Nitrogen rich chemical fertilizers clearly give tea trees a considerable boost. Nevertheless, I have tasted a few very good organic teas, so it is definitely possible to grow fine tea in a "more natural" manner. Organic farming techniques are continuously improving, and it seems inevitable that fine organic tea will become more widely available.

Another problem is that most so-called organic tea on the market is probably fake. Neither China nor Taiwan has a standard organic certification system, and various government agencies and private groups use widely differing criteria to certify foods as organic. Since organic tea fetches such a high price, unscrupulous farmers and middlemen have a considerable financial incentive to pass off regular tea as chemical-free. Hopefully a reliable and standardized certification system will emerge in the future.

Chapter 2

Tea History

The remote mountains extending from China's Yunnan Province into Burma and eastern India shielded the area from glaciers during the last ice age, a time when much of the northern hemisphere was scraped clear of flora. As a result, it remains a treasure trove of unusual primeval plants, including the tea tree. This unique plant is native to somewhere in this vast area, but was domesticated so long ago that its exact original habitat has been forgotten.

Not only is the primary habitat of tea uncertain, but we also do not even know when or how it was first consumed. Most likely tea leaves were originally mixed together with other plants and eaten or drunk as an herbal medication. Chinese physicians still prescribe tea for its healthful properties, and the healers and shamans of prehistoric mountain peoples probably pioneered its medical applications. Otherwise, in antiquity tea was most likely considered more a food than a beverage. Today people in Yunnan, northern Burma, and Thailand still consume tea leaves in salads, stews, and stir-fried dishes, often after the wet leaves have been allowed to ferment until slightly sour. These recipes seem to be survivals from an unknowably ancient cuisine.

The modern Mandarin word for tea is *cha*, but in China's numerous languages and dialects it is known by many other names such as *ming, chai, zhou, te, ti, la, chuta*. Scholars have long debated whether or not any of the plants mentioned in ancient Chinese records refer to tea, but they have yet to come to any firm conclusions. When tea-drinking started to become popular it was originally called *tu* after a bitter herb native to north China. Eventually tea became so important that it was deemed worthy of a name of its own, so *cha* replaced *tu*.

Because *tu* was the name of both tea and a completely different plant, it is difficult to pinpoint exactly when tea-drinking began in China. According to early records, ancient Chinese drank water as their primary beverage, and tea does not seem to have been consumed. Ancient Chinese probably initially encountered tea as an exotic imported medicine, and it may have been used in healing concoctions as early as the second century. Tea seems first to have gained popularity in the southernmost parts of China and gradually spread northward, so there was a time when tea-drinking was seen as a colorful southern custom. During the third century tea was being grown and consumed in parts of Yunnan, Sichuan, and Guizhou, and it steadily gained wider recognition through exports to other areas.

Members of the imperial court first regularly consumed tea during the third century, lending it new prestige. By the fourth century the beverage had made its way into mainstream Chinese culture. Growing and processing became steadily more refined, and some places became known for their high quality product. Offering tea to visitors became a common symbol of hospitality, and the rich served it to guests at luxurious banquets. Tea even started to appear in religious rituals.

As tea went into widespread cultivation far from its native habitat, farmers developed new hybrids and began cultivating trees that differed significantly from their wild ancestors. Today tea trees come in many shapes and sizes, and hybridization has allowed this plant to be grown very far north of its subtropical home. At first, tea leaves were usually processed by steaming and grinding the leaves, then compressing the resulting paste into a dried disk or some other shape. Drinking tea involved cutting off a piece of the disk, grinding the hard lump into a fine powder with a mortar, then either steeping or simmering the tea dust in hot water. Loose-leaf tea was also known at the time, although it was still uncommon.

During the mid-fourth century, Sichuan first supplied tea to the imperial court as an item of tribute. This was the beginning of the tribute tea system, an institution that had enormous influence on the development of tea technology and culture. Tea was just one item in the elaborate tribute system that supplied the emperor with luxuries difficult to obtain on the open market. Foreign countries contributed rarities such as rhinoceros horn, tropical bird feathers, and jade. Within China, each region was required to provide an annual supply of specialized local goods such as unusual foods, medicinal herbs, and opulent handicrafts. Tea became part of this system in the fourth century, and thereafter the rulers of each dynasty designated certain teas as articles of tribute. Of course, tribute tea had to be produced according to exacting standards, and innovations in court tea production gradually trickled down to influence the beverage drunk by ordinary people. The imperial court could also

Bamboo Whisk

Mortar and Grinding Wheel

dramatically alter mainstream taste by declaring a particular tea a tribute article, instantly creating enormous demand.

The Tang dynasty (618–907) was a pivotal era in tea history. When the dynasty began, tea was found primarily in southern China, but by the mid-Tang dynasty the drink had penetrated even the country's most far-flung regions. The eighth-century writer Feng Yan noted that although some people had drunk tea in previous times, in his own day the custom had become ubiquitous. The ninth-century writer Yang Hua echoed this view by remarking, "Not a day goes by without tea." For the first time tea was being grown and consumed all across China, making it a major article of both agriculture and commerce. The expansion of tea growing was probably encouraged by natural climate change, as average temperatures were somewhat warmer than in previous centuries, allowing tea to be grown farther north than ever before. So-called border tea (*biancha*) was exported in large quantities to neighboring countries during the Tang era, popularizing tea-drinking across East Asia.

The Tang emperors declared tea from sixteen regions to be items of tribute. Each variety was classified as either private or government tribute tea. Farmers handled the growing, harvest, and processing of private tribute teas themselves, whereas government tribute teas were produced under official supervision. The Tang tribute tea system was vast in scale. For example, the state factory at Huizhou spread over thirty rooms, employed 30,000 part-time *corvée* workers and a thousand professionals, and put out perhaps 100,000 disks of compressed tea each year. In addition to tea, Tang rulers also received tribute water. Pure water from Mount Hui near Wuxi was laboriously shipped an enormous distance in jugs to the imperial capital at Changan where it was used to make tea at court.

Tea came to be considered an exalted beverage during the Tang dynasty. For example, state ceremonies were adjusted to use tea instead of the alcoholic drinks that had been the norm since antiquity. Even secular court tea-drinking developed into an intricate ritual with strict rules. A formal imperial tea banquet began by burning incense to purify the air. The tea container was presented to the ruler and opened as favored courtiers looked on in anticipation, after which they scrutinized and admired the tea implements. The tea was roasted, ground, then presented to participants, who were expected to praise it with florid eulogies. Poems might even be written and chanted in praise of the leaves. Only then was the tea finally brewed and drunk.

The respected place that tea gained at court was mirrored throughout society. Originally tea was seen as an ordinary food akin to vegetable soup, and no one seems to have given it much thought. During the Tang dynasty, however, people started to look on tea as something very different from other foods and drinks. Refined gentlemen became extremely fastidious about their tea and regarded connoisseurship as an elegant pursuit. From this time forward, the most famous men of letters wrote books and poems about tea, deeming it a worthy subject for polite discourse. Literati would invite friends over for sophisticated tea parties, and the beverage was considered the ideal accompaniment for cultivated pastimes such as appreciating paintings and composing extemporaneous poetry. Although everyone now drank tea, a few connoisseurs went to enormous trouble to acquire rare tea leaves and pure water, prepare it in a faultless manner, and serve it with flair. Mastery of tea became a way publicly to demonstrate high status and cultural superiority, and sometimes the drink was prepared and appreciated in public competitions watched by large audiences.

Preparing a cup of tea was a troublesome business, and making it correctly required some skill. Paintings from the period show tea-drinkers surrounded by elaborate paraphernalia and several busy servants. The compressed leaves were usually stored in a paper wrapper, although the rich kept their tea in exquisitely crafted gold mesh containers. Tea was not yet stored in tightly sealed containers, so either metal mesh or paper protected it from contamination while allowing some contact with air. After the package was opened, a piece of the disk had to be broken off and meticulously ground to a fine powder in a mortar. A dainty, long-handled spoon was used to scoop a small amount of ground tea into a bowl, after which hot salted water was poured out from a covered pot or ewer and the tea was given time to infuse. Sometimes the powder was rapidly stirred or beaten to mix it into the water, producing surface froth which people of the time considered attractive. Drinkers swallowed the powder along with the liquid, giving early tea a potent kick. Besides salt, which was a standard ingredient, it was common to adulterate tea with other heady flavorings such as scallion, ginger, citrus peel, berries, and herbs.

Most people still brewed tea using ordinary kitchenware and drank it from the same bowls used for soup or rice. But as tea gained in popularity and prestige, craftsmen began devising special utensils. The Tang tea expert Lu Yu describes twenty-eight different kinds of tea implements. Sometimes the wealthy favored flashy luxury goods made from richly worked gold and silver. Most often, though, the elite used ceramic bowls, pots, and ewers such as serene dark celadon Yue ware or austere white Ding ware. In the early centuries of tea-drinking, fine bowls were seated on a special holder with a hole in the middle that fit the bottom of the bowl. Since servants usually made tea in a separate preparation area then carried it over to the drinker, this sort of base would have made it much easier to transport a hot bowl.

Song Dynasty Servant Heating Water

We can only wonder what this early tea tasted like. Modern Chinese green tea is usually quite light, but the ancient version was probably much stronger. The closest modern equivalent is probably the powder used in Japanese tea ceremonies. Like early Chinese tea, the Japanese product is unoxidized and finely ground. Because the Japanese still consume the powder along with the hot water, the concoction is impressively potent. However, the best Tang dynasty compressed tea was probably much better than modern Japanese powdered tea because the southern Chinese climate is so much better suited to growing this subtropical plant. And since early Chinese tea was stored in paper or mesh containers, it probably underwent some ageing, which added complexity to the flavor and aroma.

The first book dedicated to tea was the *Classic of Tea* [*Chajing*] written by the Tang connoisseur Lu Yu around 761. This book was widely read and has been reprinted innumerable times. Lu wrote intelligently on tea history, brewing techniques, and the main types of fine tea, giving us a good idea of the state of tea-drinking in the eighth century. The popularity of Lu Yu's writings established tea as a refined drink suitable for painstaking study and appreciation.

Tea also became an important fixture in the lives of Buddhist monks. Meditation is the central activity of the Buddhist faithful, who consider long periods of quiet sitting essential for obtaining the calm and insight central to Buddhist wisdom. Because tea is both relaxing and also a mild stimulant, it is the ideal drink for meditators. By consuming tea with absolute mindfulness, focusing concentration wholeheartedly on the actions of the moment, tea-drinking became elevated to a profound form of meditation. In addition, the strict rules of monastic discipline sometimes prohibited monks from eating anything after noon, so a bowl of hearty powdered tea in the afternoon could help them quell their hunger.

Some Chinese monasteries were quite wealthy in medieval times and monks became major tea consumers. According to a contemporary account, the monks at one temple drank three cups of tea after each meal. Considering the strength of early tea, this was an impressive quantity. The Buddhist clergy even became important patrons of tea culture, and some monasteries constructed special rooms for convening tea-drinking assemblies. As monks became informed patrons, they elevated tea culture by associating it closely with meditation, wisdom, and a refined body of religious aesthetics. In addition to Buddhist influence, the Daoist clergy also integrated tea-drinking into their own traditions of meditation and self-cultivation, imparting yet more spiritual significance.

Because China's climate was relatively warm during the Tang era, many prime tea-growing areas were located in north China. On average, the climate cooled somewhat during the Song dynasty (960–1279), so the center of tea cultivation shifted south once again. Although tea was grown throughout southern China during the Song dynasty, Fujian consolidated its reputation as the source of the finest tea and Song emperors declared premium Fujian tea from the Northern Garden in Jian'an an item of imperial tribute. Jian'an also sold huge quantities of good tea on the open market, and Fujian tea became a favorite of connoisseurs throughout China. Song tea buffs wrote more than two dozen books on their favorite subject, mostly about tea from Jian'an. Despite this fixation with the most famous tea appellation, a range of fine teas was grown in many places. Tea exports continued, and in 1043 alone the government oversaw the shipment of 30,000 tea disks to the Western Xia kingdom in Central Asia.

During the Song era, tea was drunk in about the same way as during the Tang period. Leaves were still usually compressed into disks or rectangles and wrapped in paper or dried bamboo leaves for protection. Some disks were coated with a layer of protective oil and had to be soaked in water then toasted dry before use. Tea was sometimes stored in tightly woven wooden baskets topped with well-fitting lids that created a tight seal, as some people now believed that tea should be kept in an airtight container. Aged tea had come to be considered undesirable, and old disks were heated over a fire to rid them of any odd flavors before grinding. Ordinary people still added fragrant dried citrus peels and spices to their tea, although the elite now looked down on this sort of adulteration.

Tribute tea was compressed into a variety of shapes including squares, ovals, hexagons, and lobed circles. The finest tribute tea was usually compressed into disks marked with an impressed dragon or phoenix. Large quantities of Song tribute tea were produced, and it was carefully classified into many grades and classes. For example, between 1098 and 1100, 1,800 pieces of compressed tribute tea were sent to court. Of course, the emperor himself drank only a tiny amount of this profusion, and he gave most of it away as a sign of imperial favor. Receiving an imperial tea disk was enormously prestigious, and serving imperial tea to guests allowed the social climber to flaunt this tangible connection with the throne.

The twelfth-century Emperor Huizong, who was particularly enthusiastic about tea, presided over competitive tastings and even wrote a book about the subject. The high standards of growing, processing, and connoisseurship cultivated at the Song court trickled down through society, raising the level of tea culture as a whole. Perhaps because Song literati were so familiar with tea, their writings seem very relaxed when compared to the stiff encomia of their solemn Tang predecessors. Many of the poems and essays about tea from this era are witty, carefree, and full of clever wordplay.

大龍
銅圈

Song Dynasty Imperial Tea Disk

Tea wares continued to evolve in beauty and sophistication. The Tang taste for ostentatious luxury was succeeded by a far more subdued aesthetic that valued quiet beauty. Although tea bowls were sometimes made of lacquer or other materials, ceramic tea ware remained the norm. As during the Tang dynasty, the bowls used by the elite rested atop special holders, although a bowl might be used by itself in informal situations. The emperor and his favorites drank tea from austere celadon Ru or Guan ware. Today some antiques experts consider these elegantly restrained pieces the finest ceramics ever made. White Ding ware maintained its appeal and was joined at court by Jun ware, which ranged in color from gray to purple.

Courtiers also began drinking tea from Jian ware bowls from Fujian, marking a major shift in tea culture away from conspicuous consumption and toward refreshingly unpretentious, natural, and even rustic taste. These simple black bowls, known in the West by the Japanese name *temmoku*, were favored by Emperor Huizong and gained popularity among the literati. Because leaves were still ground into a powder and ingested along with the water, the sides of Jian tea bowls sometimes flare out in a gentle slope, making it easier for the drinker to suck the heavy wet powder over the rim.

During the Song era, processing started to undergo a major shift as loose-leaf tea became increasingly common. Initially loose-leaf tea probably gained popularity due to the high cost of tea made from compressed disks. Because ground tea was consumed along with the liquid, the leaves could only be used for one infusion. Ground tea was costly, difficult to prepare, and also produced a severe drink. Now that tea-drinking was part of daily life, ordinary people searched for more economical and convenient methods of preparation. Loose-leaf tea caught on because the leaves could be infused several times, making it possible quickly to brew a large amount of mild tea using very few leaves. This style of tea was also much weaker than before, so it could be sipped all day.

Yuan dynasty (1279–1368) documents report that three types of tea were available at the time: loose-leaf tea, ground powder, and compressed disks. Tea disks were most expensive and prestigious, and this was still the drink of choice at the imperial court. As in the Song, tribute tea disks still came from Jian'an. However, disks had become uncommon on the open market and the average person rarely encountered them. Some people bought tea powder and drank it in the traditional fashion, but loose-leaf tea was steadily gaining ground.

Early loose-leaf tea probably tasted very different from the modern product we know. Tea leaves were originally steamed to soften them in preparation for compression, and at first farmers also processed loose-leaf tea by steaming it. Dry heat took some time to catch on. Steaming robs the leaves of flavor, so early loose-leaf tea was probably very light. During the Yuan dynasty, some farmers started processing their tea first by steaming then by roasting the leaves. People soon realized that steaming was unnecessary, and the technique died out. Because these leaves were more potent, fewer were required, so this innovation made loose-leaf tea even less expensive for consumers. Once farmers began processing loose-leaf tea with dry heat instead of steam, the modern beverage was born.

During the Ming dynasty (1368–1644), tea-drinking took on an appearance that seems familiar to us today. At the beginning of the dynasty, tribute disks were still being sent to the imperial court. Emperor Taizu, the dynasty's founder, was born a commoner and probably grew up drinking loose-leaf tea, so he abolished the unfamiliar tea disks soon after ascending the throne. From that time forward, imperial tea was similar to the drink consumed by wealthy merchants and literati. The Ming emperors also abolished many of the tiresome rituals and luxurious accoutrements surrounding tea-drinking, preferring to enjoy it in a more relaxed fashion.

Although Taizu banished tea disks from court, they were still favored by various peoples along China's long borders from Yunnan to Tibet and up through Mongolia. Although disks had previously been looked up to as an elegant courtly drink, they were now primarily associated with marginal ethnic groups, leading most Chinese to regard this sort of tea as an inferior product. Even today many of the peoples along China's southern and western borders have maintained their taste for compressed tea and preserve some archaic Chinese tea-drinking customs.

During the Ming, tea was almost always made by steeping loose leaves inside a pot or covered cup. When a pot was used, tea was usually poured into tiny cups for drinking. Processing also continued to evolve. Steaming mostly died out, and leaves were prepared by heating them over a fire or inside an oven. As processing techniques improved, tea became ever more varied and subtle. A sixteenth-century book on tea lists ninety-seven types, and there were undoubtedly many lesser kinds as well. Ming tribute tea came from Jianning in Fujian, the same region that formerly produced tea disks, but farmers there now provided loose-leaf green tea for the monarch. The Ming court continued the Tang custom of using tribute water to brew their tea, although they shipped in water from a much closer source called Jade Spring near Beijing, a practice continued by rulers of the subsequent Qing dynasty.

Loose-leaf tea required new and completely different kinds of tea ware. This transition in drinking methods was an epochal event in the history of Chinese ceramics, stimulating the invention of new styles and technologies. Although southern Chinese had sometimes used teapots in earlier eras, during the Ming the teapot became the standard vessel for brewing tea. Generally speaking, there were originally two basic styles of teapot. Those from Yixing, crafted from brown clay in simple shapes, kept alive the Song aesthetic of austere simplicity and naturalism. The refined understatement of these pieces appealed to sophisticated literati. In contrast, both the imperial court and prosperous merchants favored more polished ceramics. Besides white Dehua ware, the Ming was the golden age of delicate blue and white porcelain.

The nomadic Manchus who conquered China and established the Qing dynasty (1644–1911) enthusiastically embraced Chinese tea culture. The Qing emperors were very cosmopolitan in this regard and patronized teas from many areas besides Fujian. At one point, teas from forty-six areas were declared items of imperial tribute. The monarch usually drank loose-leaf tea, including some varieties still famous today such as *biluo* spring, *longjing*, and Wuyi.

Tea disks also made a minor comeback, albeit in altered form. Because the Manchus were originally nomads, they were accustomed to eating large quantities of fatty meat. This hearty diet could easily cause indigestion, so the Qing rulers started drinking compressed *puer* tea from Yunnan in winter because of its renowned digestive properties. The emperors sometimes even consumed this tea with salt and milk in the fashion of nomadic peoples. However, this new compressed tea was entirely different from earlier court disk tea. Song and Yuan emperors preferred disks of green tea made from ordinary small-leaf trees grown in the prime tea region of Fujian. In contrast, *puer* is made from the leaves of big-leaf feral trees from Yunnan, traditionally considered a marginal tea appellation, and at some point the leaves started to be fully oxidized. Although both kinds of tea were pressed into disks, the flavor, in fact, was entirely different. Most importantly, compressed leaves were no longer ground into a powder and consumed along with the water. Instead, a chunk of the disk was broken off and steeped in a pot like loose-leaf tea. *Puer* was originally a humble brew consumed by ethnic minorities in Yunnan and other border areas, but after being adopted at court it gained a following among tea cognoscenti. Nevertheless, compressed tea remained a specialized product and loose leaves were still the norm.

Mainstream Qing taste in tea decisively rejected the Song emphasis on muted simplicity. Ceramic technology progressed enormously during the final centuries of the imperial era, and potters were eager to show off their virtuosity. Flamboyant colors and unusual shapes were the order of the day. Discerning literati kept alive the taste for austere Yixing ware, but sometimes potters could not resist gilding the lily and enameled even these simple pieces with incongruously bright flowers and butterflies. Demand from the flamboyant Qing court fed the mania for gaudy colors, and extravagantly enameled pots and cups became the norm throughout China.

Tea culture became more creative than ever. New teas proliferated and most of the famous varieties we drink today emerged in their modern form at this time. Farmers experimented with oxidation, inventing oolongs and red teas. Tea leaves were aged and blended with flowers. A sixteenth-century author lists dozens of dried flowers that were being mixed with tea, including fragrant exotica such as lotus petals and gardenia blossoms. Commerce in tea also became more sophisticated, and shopkeepers and middlemen frequently collaborated with ambitious farmers to invent new styles of tea. Even the smallest town had a teahouse, and these lively venues were the most popular place for men to meet friends, conduct business, hear the latest news, find a prostitute, and listen to musicians and storytellers.

In this era tea became a major commodity worldwide as China exported huge quantities to countries across the globe. Fujian was one of the first places to sell tea to the West. In the local Hokkien dialect, tea is pronounced *dei*. This was initially written in roman letters as *ti*, and the English spelled this strange-looking foreign word "tea" (originally pronounced "tay"). Not only did Europeans buy tea from China, but they also imported Chinese pots, and the earliest Western-made teapots resembled Chinese prototypes. These were often quite small by today's standards, and, in fact, they were very well suited for brewing tea. Over time Western teapots steadily grew in size until they reached the unwieldy dimensions of today.

Foreign and domestic tastes were extremely different, so exports had a significant impact on the development of Chinese tea. Initially, merchants tended to export the sort of teas that local people enjoyed, but as foreigners became more familiar with tea they started to express their own preferences. The biggest change came in the nineteenth century when foreign drinkers became partial to heavily oxidized tea. This sort of tea travels well, making it ideal for long ocean voyages to distant markets. Large-scale exports from British tea plantations in India and Ceylon, which produced oxidized "English" tea, were also influential in shaping Western tastes. Britain was the superpower of the day, so anything English was emulated around the world. The British patriotically drank plantation-grown oxidized tea from their colonies, and consumers elsewhere followed their lead. Hefty teapots became standard in the West, and delicate varieties of Chinese tea taste watery and flavorless when brewed in these capacious monsters. Once Western teapots expanded to the point that they were only good for brewing strongly flavored tea, the world hegemony of dark English tea (tarted up with lots of milk and sugar) was assured.

In 1874, almost 3.5 million pounds of oolong tea were exported from Fujian to the United States, but by 1899 this had dropped to less than 32,000 pounds. Within a few decades, most Westerners had lost interest in Chinese tea. Farmers and merchants struggled to adjust to these seismic shifts in the export market. Although domestic demand for red tea was small, this variety nevertheless went into widespread cultivation across southern China as an export product. Even so, enormous British colonial tea plantations benefited from economies of scale and standardized processing, so China struggled to compete with South Asia in the cutthroat export market.

The twentieth century brought terrible hardships to China, and the tea industry suffered as well. For decades the country was torn apart by civil war and foreign invasions. Many people were so impoverished that they could not even afford a daily pot of tea, so farmers abandoned long-cultivated fields and some varieties became extinct. The 1949 Communist revolution had even bigger ramifications for the industry. In 1954, tea was brought under the new system of central planning that aimed to standardize production and match output with national needs. Communist cadres initially viewed tea as an expendable luxury. As they forced farmers to switch to edible crops, tea production plummeted. In 1958, Chairman Mao Zedong, an enthusiastic tea-drinker, proclaimed that more tea ought to be grown on hillside slopes as a way of using marginal farmland, so production leveled off.

Under communism, nihilistic political campaigns took a heavy toll on tea output and quality. The state forcefully collectivized agriculture and dragooned peasants into communes, discouraging individual initiative and quality control. During 1958–60 the Great Leap Forward campaign mobilized China's masses to increase agricultural production, and much of the growing and processing of tea was done by unmotivated amateurs such as teachers, students, and office workers. Tea production suffered further during the chaos of the Cultural Revolution (1966–76). In 1965, Yunnan Province exported almost 7 million pounds of tea, but by 1973 this had dwindled to just 27,000 pounds.

Quality suffered enormously under central planning. Because communist ideologues regarded commerce with suspicion, tea middlemen lived in constant fear of being denounced as capitalist roaders. It was also politically suspect to stress quality instead of quantity, so famous tea fields declined into weedy mediocrity. Chinese consumers bought tea that was neither identified by region nor graded by quality. The good, bad, and awful were haphazardly thrown together and sold under generic labels. On communes and in factories, production methods steadily regressed as revolutionaries arrogantly disregarded the hard-won wisdom gained from centuries of experience. Central planners sought only to churn out a slapdash beverage sufficient to slake the thirst of the laboring masses. Moreover, inefficient state enterprises monopolized tea exports, offering foreign customers an uncertain product and poor service. Of course, this system could not possibly match their efficient competition in South Asia, so tea from India and Sri Lanka (as Ceylon had become) continued to reign supreme on the world market.

Fortunately, the story of Chinese tea has a happy ending. Revolted by the chaos and poverty of the Cultural Revolution, in the 1980s the Chinese people decisively turned their backs on central planning. Under the new free market system, farmers once again tilled their own fields, giving them the incentive to work hard and raise quality. Tea production skyrocketed, and in the last few years China has once again regained its rightful place as the world's biggest tea exporter. Processing and marketing have also opened up to free competition, further raising quality and guaranteeing nimble responses to market demand. Rapid economic development has created a large new Chinese middle class that is prosperous, educated, and sophisticated, spurring an unprecedented demand for fine tea. China's major cities are now dotted with elegant teahouses and well-appointed teashops. Never before has so much good tea in so many varieties been so widely available. How lucky we are to be living at the dawn of the golden age of Chinese tea!

Song Dynasty Jun Ware Bowl and Stand

Chapter 3

How to Drink Tea

Because tea-drinking has such a long history, we are the lucky heirs to centuries of practical wisdom. Chinese experts have steadily refined tea preparation through centuries of trial and error, and generations of experienced drinkers have passed down their tea-making secrets. Learning these sophisticated techniques will maximize quality and heighten appreciation, giving you the most pleasure from your tea. Our tea-drinking forefathers discovered that white and green teas should usually be prepared in a covered bowl, a very simple method described at the end of this chapter. Most other teas taste best when prepared in a small pot, and brewing tea this way is far more involved.

What follows is a description of the most elaborate way to prepare a pot of tea in the Chinese style. Of course, no one will go through every step of this model routine for each cup. Sometimes it is best just to forget about appreciation and drink tea informally as nothing more than a pleasant beverage. Even when consciously savoring tea, connoisseurship should never lapse into affectation. Chinese tea-lovers often mock the Japanese tea ceremony for its picayune rules and tiresome rituals. In contrast with stern Japanese formality, Chinese tea-drinking embodies a far more natural aesthetic. Whenever you drink tea, remember to relax, be yourself, and enjoy the moment. Any trace of fussiness or pretension violates the free and easy Daoist spirit that makes Chinese tea-drinking so enjoyable.

This being said, sometimes it is very useful to drink tea in the traditional style with careful attention to detail. This is not an arbitrary ritual, but merely a time-tested way to brew the very best tea and enjoy it as much as possible. Following the steps outlined below will increase understanding and enjoyment of every nuance of the experience. You might find some of these procedures so pleasing and useful that you will want to add them to your everyday drinking routine. Other steps might be reserved for special occasions when you want to drink a new or special tea with exceptional sensitivity to taste and aroma.

Here at the outset, I should emphasize a key point: it is infinitely more convenient to use the metric system instead of the Fahrenheit one when discussing tea. The ideal temperature for brewing each kind of tea differs considerably. The water for heavily oxidized varieties like Fujian oolongs, red, and black teas should be close to boiling, while green and white tea should be steeped in water no hotter more than about two-thirds boiling. Few will bother to dip a thermometer into a teapot, so if I say that your tea water should be 170° F, this information is not particularly useful. Even most physicists would not be able to estimate water temperature in Fahrenheit by sight. In contrast to the complicated Fahrenheit system, the Celsius scale so simple that you can easily learn to estimate temperature just by looking at the water. Water boils at 100° centigrade. This means that 90° is nine-tenths boiling, 80° is eight-tenths boiling, and so on. By thinking of tea-water temperature in centigrade terms, it is much easier to judge what is happening in your teapot by sight and to brew your tea at the proper temperature.

Yixing Teapots

Tea brewed in a small teapot is called *gongfu* tea, a term usually spelled *kung fu* in English. Although most people associate *kung fu* with Hong Kong chop-sockey movies, in fact, this term doesn't refer specifically to the martial arts. In Chinese the word *gongfu* is used to describe anything done exceptionally well. Tea brewed in a small pot is called *gongfu* because Chinese tea-drinkers universally agree that this is the best way to do it. Preparing tea this way is admittedly time consuming and requires some effort, but the results are well worth the trouble. Some people refer to it as "old person's tea" because drinking tea from a small pot is a common pastime among Chinese retirees who have the free time to brew their tea the best way possible.

Instead of seeing this meticulous method of preparation as a hindrance, you should look at it as a positive addition to your life. How many times have you seen someone absentmindedly sipping takeout coffee from a paper cup while rushing to an appointment? Does this sort of drinking experience add anything constructive to life? Chinese refer to people like that as "headless flies"—the sort of people who go buzzing through life without ever noticing what's around them. In contrast,

Yixing Teapot, Tall Sniffing Cup, and Squat Drinking Cup

patiently sitting and waiting for tea to brew is the perfect excuse to put aside your multi-tasking and relax for a change. Because *gongfu* tea forces you to slow down and smell the roses, it is a welcome antidote to the stresses of modern life.

Unlike the ideal Chinese teapot, a large Western-style pot is fantastically wasteful. It requires a large quantity of leaves to produce watery third-rate tea. The golden rule of tea-drinking is very simple: the smaller the pot, the better the tea. A small pot concentrates flavor in a confined space, gives the drinker maximum control over the brewing process, and also requires very few leaves. Without question, the small teapots from Yixing (pronounced *ee-shing*) are the world's finest. Although each of these vessels is precisely handcrafted by a master potter, a simple Yixing pot only costs a few dollars or a couple pounds. Considering their superb design and craftsmanship, practicality, beauty, and low cost, Yixing teapots are one of the greatest bargains around. Anyone who gets used to drinking tea from an Yixing pot will inevitably start to despise outsized Western teapots as wasteful and awkward behemoths.

Yixing is a historic city in the Yangtze River basin long famous for its ceramics. Just mention this town and any Chinese person will smile and start to talk about teapots. Yixing ware is made from a remarkable clay called purple sand (*zisha*). Despite the name, this clay comes in various shades ranging from dark red to brown and black. Purple sand clay is what the English potter Josiah Wedgwood (1730–95) was trying to imitate when he created his famous jasperware. Purple sand clay is so pleasant to the touch that Yixing pots do not need a glaze. When burnished and fired at a low temperature, this miraculous material becomes smooth and glossy yet somewhat porous. Any water or tea dribbled on the surface is quickly sucked into the walls. If used regularly, an Yixing pot will eventually absorb a fair amount of tea oil and develop a shiny patina. At that point, just adding hot water to an empty seasoned pot will yield a very weak tea produced from the accumulated oil.

During the eleventh century, potters around Yixing first began crafting teapots. Tasteful gentlemen across China soon recognized their virtuosity and used them to brew tea. Today Yixing pots come in an infinite variety of shapes, and collectors seek out creative pieces or works by famous master potters. Although the basic design adheres to tradition, these simple pots still look very stylish and modern. It is a waste of money to buy antique Yixing ware as these pieces are easily faked. Yixing pots that are well-balanced, pour without dribbling, and shine with an attractive patina are inexpensive and easy to find.

When choosing a teapot, utility is paramount. Practicality does not preclude beauty, however, as the most functional handmade Yixing teapots are almost always very attractive as well. Most importantly, be sure to select a small pot. The body of a standard Yixing pot is about the size of a fist. When making tea for one or two people, if you're not in any hurry it's best to use an even smaller pot. A miniature pot with a body about two inches in diameter gives maximum control over the leaves.

Before buying an Yixing teapot, rub a finger along the interior walls. If these are slightly rough on the inside, you know that the pot was probably made by hand. Handmade pieces have far more character than the bland replicas cast in molds. Next, try to jiggle the lid. The lid of a well-made teapot should fit snugly onto the body, producing a tight seal. You should also ask the merchant to put some water into the pot and let you pour it out. A good teapot feels comfortable and well-balanced in the hand when full, and the liquid should exit the spout in a smooth arc without any dribbling. Not every teapot pours well, and few things in life are more exasperating than a teapot that dribbles.

Before Brewing

Tea appreciation begins well before tasting the first drop. If you know some basic facts about a tea before you drink it, the experience will be more meaningful. The staff of a decent teashop should be able to explain quite a bit about their goods. If they cannot answer your questions, buy your tea somewhere else. At the very least, find out where a tea is from, its basic characteristics, and the degree of oxidation.

If you own many kinds of tea, it helps to note when and where the leaves were purchased. Store leaves properly in airtight containers kept in a dark place. Most stored tea will degrade quickly if exposed to sunlight or humidity. It should be easy to crush the dry tea leaves into a powder between two fingers. Leaves that feel rubbery and resist crushing when rubbed together have probably absorbed a harmful dose of humidity. If a tea has dramatically changed color or smell since its purchase, it may have gone bad.

Before brewing, observe the dry leaves carefully. Are they whole or chopped? If the leaves are whole, pay attention to the shape, which can vary quite a bit. Tea leaves can be large or small and have either pointed or rounded ends. The shape of the leaf reveals which sort of tree it came from. Leaves are often crinkled or rolled into balls, affecting intensity and rhythm. Some teas are made from only young sprouts, others from old leaves, while most mix together sprouts and mature leaves in varying proportions. The maturity of the leaves affects quality and strength. Has the tea been compressed into a disk or brick? If so, note its dimensions, weight, and packaging. Notice any other relevant characteristics that will affect the final brew, such as the proportion of stems to leaves, any additives such as flowers, or the presence of any foreign matter.

Next, examine the color and texture of the leaves. Most importantly, the color of the leaves usually reveals the degree of oxidation. Generally speaking, the darker the leaf the more oxidation it has undergone. To the trained eye, the color and shape of the leaf also disclose many clues about processing. Roasting, baking, rolling, crushing, steaming, and sun drying each leave behind telltale signs. Ageing or improper storage can sometimes show up as white powder, yellow mildew, green mildew, spots of mold, or white spider-web patterns.

Finally, take some time to appreciate the aroma of the dry leaves. This fragrance is quite different from the smell the leaves will exude after being soaked in hot water. It is useful to compare the aromas of dry and wet tea leaves because faint odors barely detectable in one can be much more prominent in the other. The smell exuded by most leaves is actually a heady mix of numerous individual fragrances, so try to single out some of the main components. These smells are easier to think about and remember if you give them names based on familiar odors they resemble, such as flowers and fruits.

Brewing

Most people put their Yixing pot in a broad shallow bowl to keep the table dry while they are pouring water in and out. A bowl is also a convenient place to dump excess water and used leaves, and any hot waste water in the bowl will help keep the pot warm. In addition to a teapot and shallow bowl, the standard equipment includes sniffing cups, tasting cups, a decanter, and a kettle. Other specialized tea implements may not be absolutely necessary, but they can come in handy: a scoop for getting the dry leaves into the pot; a squat funnel that fits into the mouth of the pot to guide the leaves inside; a slop pot for excess water and used leaves; large wooden tweezers to pull used leaves out of the pot; and a pointed stick for dislodging any stray tea leaves that clog the spout.

Because a petite Yixing pot does not make much tea with each infusion, small cups are most appropriate. A small cup also encourages the drinker to slow down and savor each sip. Formal tasting uses two kinds of very small cups, one for sniffing, the other for drinking. A sniffing cup is relatively tall and narrow while the cup for drinking is squat and broad. The sniffing cup has a small mouth and is about 2 inches high, while the broad-mouthed drinking-cup is only about 1 inch high. Drinking cups should have a white porcelain interior, because only a neutral background can show off the tea's true color.

A decanter is used to hold the tea after it is poured out of the pot but before it is poured into the cups. This vessel is usually ceramic and ought to be about the same volume as the pot. A decanter needs a wide mouth to receive tea from the pot and a flared rim or spout to pour tea into the cups without spilling. When the tea in the pot has infused to optimal strength, pour it into the decanter. This stops the brewing process at precisely the right moment. Otherwise the tea would keep stewing away in the pot until the drinkers happen to empty their cups, and the next round of tea might be too strong. Pouring tea into the cups from the decanter instead of the pot also ensures that each drinker's tea is exactly the same strength.

As for the kettle, this can be made of metal, ceramic, or glass. Some drinkers prefer large kettles; others use a small one. A small kettle gives most control over water temperature and is fast to heat up, although of course one has to keep adding new water and warming it up again. I like old Japanese iron kettles, which are both beautiful and utilitarian. Some Chinese tea-drinkers complain that Japanese kettles give the water an iron taste, although I have never found this to be a problem. It is also possible to use two kettles, a large utilitarian one to heat water on the stove, and a smaller and more decorative one to bring hot water to the table. Serious tea-drinkers often heat a kettle at the table over an electric element or alcohol flame to monitor water temperature constantly. For ultimate convenience, an electric water heater keeps the water inside just below the boiling-point. A well-insulated thermos is also handy.

To begin brewing, first pour some hot water into the empty Yixing pot, allow it sit for a few seconds, and then pour the water off into the cups and decanter. Besides washing and sterilizing all the tea implements, this also warms up the pot, decanter, and cups so that the tea will remain hot longer as it sits. Chinese teapots and cups are so small that the tea inside tends to cool quickly. It is especially important to warm the pot and cups in winter or else you will probably end up drinking iced tea. Some tea-drinkers also pour hot water over the outside of the pot to warm up the exterior. In other words, regardless of how you do it, use hot water to wash and warm up all the vessels you will be using to brew and drink the tea. The excess water will collect around the teapot in the shallow bowl.

Next, add leaves to the pot. There are specialized scoops and funnels for this, some quite elegant, although a humble tablespoon does the job about as well. The amount of leaves depends on the kind of tea, and knowing how much of each type to use comes only with experience. For most teas you will want to cover the bottom of an Yixing teapot with a thin layer of leaves. Use more leaves if they are flat, as these will expand least. If leaves are crinkled, use fewer. Balled tea requires the fewest leaves, as each ball will expand to surprisingly large dimensions. The number of leaves has a major impact on the final taste. Using too few leaves will make the tea watery and insipid. Using too many is not only wasteful but also counterproductive, because if the expanded leaves are packed together too tightly the water cannot circulate and the tea will not infuse properly.

After scooping some leaves into the warm pot, close the lid and wait for about a minute. The warmth of the pot will cause the dry leaves to release a burst of fragrance. Open the lid and sniff. If the tea is good, the aroma should be sweet and intoxicating. After savoring this perfume, fill the pot with hot water and replace the lid. Contrary to what most people think, tea water should not always be heated to boiling. In fact, excessively hot water will cause many teas to release objectionable flavors. Ideal water temperature varies considerably depending upon the type of tea to be brewed. The general rule of thumb is that the more heavily oxidized the tea, the hotter the water. Yellow tea takes water from about 75°–80° C (165°–175° F). Taiwan oolongs are usually brewed at about 85°–90° C (185°–195° F) while darker Fujian oolongs take water just below boiling. Fully oxidized red and black tea can be brewed with boiling water.

Many people pour some hot water into the pot then immediately dump it out to "wash the leaves." There is a practical reason for this custom. Tea is often grown and processed in very poor rural areas under less than pristine conditions. I have seen piles of tea sitting on cement floors, freshly picked leaves drying in baskets beside dusty roads, and leaves being hand processed by distracted children as they watch cartoons on television. Anyone who has witnessed what can happen to tea before it gets into a clean shiny tin will want to rinse the leaves as a hygienic precaution. In addition to producing a sterile beverage, washing the leaves will also remove any soot, dust, stray leaf fragments, and residual pesticides.

After washing the tea, pour more hot water onto it and allow the leaves to sit. In some parts of China, people hold the kettle high above the pot as they pour, claiming that this stirs the leaves around and wets them evenly. However, if you are not very experienced, you will probably end up pouring hot water on the table. The steeping time depends upon the size of the pot, the type and amount of leaves, the water temperature, and how many times the leaves have been infused. The more highly oxidized the tea, the faster it brews. In a small pot the first infusion of a heavy red tea will be ready in 30 seconds, while yellow tea might take several minutes to infuse properly. A chunk of compressed tea will also take a few minutes to soften up and start infusing. Of course each subsequent infusion takes longer. Try doubling

Song Dynasty Tea Drinking

the steeping time of each infusion of a new tea and see how this works. If the tea is too strong or weak, adjust the steeping time accordingly.

If you pour tea directly from pot to cups, each cup of tea will have a slightly different strength. Therefore, when the tea has brewed to proper strength, pour the contents of the entire pot into the decanter. From the decanter, first pour some tea into the tall sniffing cups, then pour it from the sniffing cups into the drinking cups. Sniffing cups are never used to drink tea. Instead, put your nose inside the mouth of the empty sniffing cup and inhale. This vessel's tall narrow shape concentrates the lingering aroma, creating an intense olfactory experience that connoisseurs call cold aroma. Not only is it extremely pleasurable, but cold aroma is also very useful as it mimics the tea's "throat." Cold aroma is a concentrated facsimile of the vapors that waft upward inside your throat and to the sinuses after you swallow a mouthful of tea. The cold aroma of good tea is extremely potent and sweet. Commonsense would suggest that the aroma ought to be strongest right after the tea is poured out of the sniffing cup, but this is not the case. The fragrance unexpectedly continues to build for up to a minute after the cup has been emptied. Sniff the cup several times to appreciate how the cold aroma develops over time: once immediately after it has been poured out, again about 30 seconds later, and one last time after about a minute.

Before tasting the tea, note the color and fragrance of the liquid as it sits in the drinking cup. Attentively sip the brew, contemplating the various component flavors and how the liquid tastes in different parts of the mouth. To appreciate tea fully, your drinking should be deliberate and thoughtful. About three-fourths of the caffeine is extracted from the leaf in the first 30 seconds, so the first infusion carries the most punch. Other aroma and flavor compounds leach out much more slowly, so each infusion has somewhat different aromas and flavors. When the drinking cup is empty, you can sniff it to savor the cold aroma. This is a good way to pass the time while waiting for the next batch of tea to finish brewing.

When the decanter is empty, add more water to the pot and repeat the process. After the first infusion, most drinkers skip the sniffing cups and pour tea from the decanter directly into the drinking cups. The number of times a batch of leaves can be infused depends on their quality, the size of the pot, and the type of tea. In a small pot, fine leaves can usually be infused three or four times, while exceptional tea can be infused six or seven times.

After Drinking

After drinking the final infusion, dump or scoop the leaves out of the pot. It is easiest to do this with special wooden tongs that resemble giant tweezers, although a finger will also get the job done. Before discarding the leaves, spread them out and examine them carefully to note their size, shape, color, degree of expansion, and texture. Observing used leaves reveals quite a bit about the tea and can also help you decide how many leaves to use next time. Because used tea leaves are so expressive, connoisseurs often dump them into a special bowl next to the pot for everyone at the table to examine.

Wash off the pot, tools, and cups with nothing more than hot water. Never use soap to clean tea ware. Many of the implements used to brew tea are highly porous, and terracotta, wood, or bamboo will instantly soak up any noxious chemicals. The flavor of tea is so delicate that even minute amounts of detergent will contaminate subsequent batches. Soap will also instantly ruin the subtle patina of a carefully seasoned Yixing pot. Destroying a carefully nurtured patina with soap would be a monstrous travesty, and ruining someone's teapot this way would test even the strongest friendships.

You may want to season your Yixing pot a bit before putting it away. Purple sand clay is extremely porous and readily absorbs oil from the tea. If you use an Yixing pot regularly, tea oil will gradually leach into the clay and give it an attractive patina. The shine that comes from years of accumulated tea oil brings out the inner beauty of the clay, and connoisseurs consider a shiny patina extremely desirable. A well-seasoned Yixing pot always elicits nods of appreciation from informed tea-drinkers.

Although seasoning occurs naturally over time, you can speed up the process. As you drink, occasionally pour a bit of tea on top of the pot. You can also use a clean soft Chinese calligraphy brush or paintbrush to sweep tea over the pot's surface repeatedly. After each stroke, the clay will quickly absorb the liquid. Getting more tea into the pot's walls this way speeds up seasoning.

For those who have more money than patience, there is another option. If you visit China, a trip to a flea market might yield a magnificently seasoned old Yixing pot that someone's grandfather used for decades. Buying a vintage pot is the fastest way to acquire one with a handsome finish. You should be cautious, however, as unscrupulous antique dealers know how to give an Yixing pot an artificial patina by boiling it in water mixed with a bit of processed tea oil.

Other Ways to Drink Tea

Besides brewing tea in a Yixing teapot, there are several other ways to enjoy the beverage, all of them quite popular. China is an enormous country, and tea-drinking customs vary considerably from place to place. Yixing pots are particularly popular in Jiangsu, Fujian, and Taiwan, but other customs often prevail elsewhere. Moreover, small teapots are not appropriate for every kind of tea.

Westerners customarily brew tea in a large pot, and this method is popular in parts of China as well. The Cantonese are especially fond of large teapots, perhaps due to British influence. As soon as diners in Hong Kong or Guangzhou sit down in a restaurant, a waiter immediately offers them their choice of several kinds of tea. A large pot sits on the table throughout the meal, and diners periodically remove the lid to let the staff know when to add hot water. A big pot is convenient when tea is nothing more than an everyday beverage to accompany food. Heavily oxidized varieties such as black and red tea can usually stand up to a large pot. If you brew green tea or Taiwan oolong this way, however, most of the nuance will be lost and you will be drinking little more than lightly scented water.

To brew tea in a large pot Chinese-style, first rinse it with hot water. This not only cleans the interior but also heats it up so that the tea will stay warm longer. Next, scoop some leaves into the warmed pot. If you like, you can replace the lid and let the leaves warm up inside for a minute, then uncover it and enjoy the resulting aroma. Next, fill the teapot with hot water and replace the lid. As with a small pot, the higher the degree of oxidation the hotter the water should be. After all the tea has been drunk, you can usually add more water to the leaves if you are using good tea. In the better Hong Kong restaurants, the tea sometimes comes to the table in a big pot that does not contain any leaves. In this case the tea is brewed to perfect strength in the kitchen and waiters bring it to the table in a special serving-pot. This clever custom solves one of the main problems with large pots, which is lack of control over the strength of the brew.

Tea can also be brewed in a covered cup, the standard custom in Beijing and other parts of north China. Green and white tea is best brewed in a covered cup, as a teapot concentrates the acrid flavors usually present in unoxidized teas. Brewing cups are fairly large and come with a cover to keep the tea hot while it steeps. These cups usually lack handles but have a large flared rim at the top and a saucer on the bottom, giving the drinker two ways to pick up the hot cup. The design of these cups is ingenious. Not only do they feel very comfortable in the hand and perform their job admirably, but they are also quite elegant in appearance. Although brewing cups are traditionally made of fine porcelain, glass cups are now available. These allow one to appreciate the beauty of the leaves as they dance and unfold in the hot water.

Although traditional brewing teacups are graceful and practical, in daily life most Chinese make do with a large handled cup that resembles a tall mug with a cover. Although usually ugly, a covered mug is nevertheless extremely practical. This vessel is stable and easy to grasp, and the cover and thick walls keep the tea warm for a long time. Of course, since covered mugs are so large, the tea will not taste nearly as good as when it is brewed in a traditional brewing teacup.

To make tea in a covered mug, first rinse out the vessel with hot water to clean and warm it. Next, add some tea leaves. Usually it is sufficient barely to cover the bottom of the cup with leaves. Pour in hot water and replace the lid to keep the tea hot while it brews. If you are brewing green tea, remember not to use water that is too close to boiling. Drinkers remove the lid when taking a sip, then replace it to keep the tea warm while it sits. When you finish, more hot water can usually be added to the leaves, and decent tea is good for several infusions if it does not sit too long each time.

When drinking from a large brewing teacup or covered mug, the leaves can sometimes become a nuisance. Some leaves sink, others float, and the most energetic repeatedly sink then float back to the surface. If you are drinking a floating tea in polite company, it is considered good form to use the lid of your teacup gently to brush the leaves to one side, clearing an empty space for your mouth to get to the liquid underneath. Chinese are an admirably pragmatic people, and blowing on tea to cool it down or push the leaves out of the way is not considered rude.

In China, a covered mug can be found on nearly every desk. Photographs of Chinese officials inevitably show rows of stiffly posed seated apparatchiks with identical covered tea cups lined up in front of them. This sort of workhorse office tea usually sits there all day, slowly stewing away from morning till evening. Some people drink this tea very weak, adding just a few token leaves to give the water a hint of flavor. Others use more leaves or change them periodically throughout the day to make stronger tea. Chinese employers are often expected to provide an unlimited supply of cheap tea leaves for their employees, and many offices have a closet-like tearoom off to one corner where employees repeatedly go for tea leaves and hot water. This inevitably becomes the main space for socializing, as everyone in the office makes numerous pilgrimages there throughout the day to obtain hot water and the latest gossip. Of course, tea made this way is far from ideal, but it still tastes much better than most other beverages and is certainly much healthier than soft drinks.

Another method for brewing tea uses a covered cup as a makeshift teapot. Tea is brewed inside a large covered cup then poured out into tiny teacups (of the sort used with an Yixing pot) for drinking. The key is to open the lid just a crack to allow tea to pour out while keeping the leaves inside. People in the area around Shantou and some other places routinely brew tea this way. Also, many connoisseurs throughout China like this technique because it gives a very high degree of control over the leaves, and it is probably the optimal way to brew green tea. However, making tea this way is not at all easy and requires dexterity and practice.

To use a cup like a teapot, first rinse out a large covered porcelain teacup with hot water and add some leaves. Use the same number of leaves as you would for a pot the same size. Next, pour in hot water and replace the lid. Now comes the hard part. When the tea is brewed to proper strength, lift up the cup by the flared rim and arrange the cover so it is open just a crack along one side. Pour the tea through this thin gap into small drinking cups. This is much harder than it looks. If you miscalculate, nothing will come out at all or else a torrent of tea will pour out onto the table and you will scald your fingers. When the tea has been consumed you can add more water to the covered cup, just as you would with an Yixing pot.

A final brewing method employs a soup bowl and large spoon. Although most Chinese have never even heard of making tea this way, it's frequently used at professional tea tastings. This may not be a very aesthetic way to drink tea, but it's very fast and allows ambitious drinkers to sample a dozen or more teas in ninety minutes. This method requires a Chinese soup bowl (much smaller but taller than a Western soup bowl), a broad porcelain Chinese soup spoon, and tiny teacups of the sort used with an Yixing pot. First rinse out the bowl and teacups with hot water and add leaves to the bowl. If you like, you can invert a second bowl on top of the main one and hold it there for 30 seconds or so to concentrate the aroma, then open it up and sniff the warmed dry leaves inside. Next, add water to the bowl and insert the porcelain spoon. Once the tea has brewed to proper strength, spoon some liquid into the teacups and drink. Be sure to sniff the spoon, as it concentrates the aroma wonderfully and gives an excellent idea of the tea's throat. You might want to use this method at home to compare several closely related teas or even host a tea-tasting party for like-minded friends.

Chapter 4

Tea Appreciation

The day you realize the profundity of the delicious liquid steaming in your cup, you become a tea connoisseur. Experiencing tea to the fullest extent requires knowledge and awareness, so educated appreciation places some demands on the drinker. Taste, aroma, density, color, leaf shape, and other variables can be divided and subdivided into innumerable gradations. Although only professionals will want to make the very finest distinctions, anyone can benefit from learning the basic principles of tea appreciation. While these details may seem daunting at first glance, with experience they become second nature and fade into the subconscious. Once you internalize this basic knowledge, whenever you encounter an unfamiliar brew you will know how to approach it intelligently. At that point, the basic background information will automatically inform your appreciation, and you can devote your attention simply to enjoying the delicious drink in front of you.

Tea appreciation is far more than just a physical experience occurring on the tongue. In fact, enjoying tea takes place primarily in the mind. The same tea can seem very different to two people, and your environment, mood, beliefs, preconceptions, expectations, experience, companions, habits, and knowledge all influence how a tea tastes to you. Serious tea-drinkers carefully regulate these subjective features by seeking out congenial company and elegant surroundings to heighten their psychological experience. Ideally, tea appreciation is just one component of an all-encompassing aesthetic. Chinese connoisseurs have always understood that tea tastes better when relaxing on a lazy afternoon, sitting at a comfortably worn antique table, gazing at a beautiful flower arrangement, listening to quiet music, and engaging a few good friends in interesting conversation. At its highest level, tea connoisseurship goes far beyond the beverage itself to become the foundation of a supremely civilized way of life.

Chinese also believe that drinking tea fosters deep camaraderie and can even bring about spiritual insight. Unlike most beverages, which can be slammed down quickly, brewing tea takes time. If you use a small Yixing pot and premium tea, a large pinch of leaves can easily last an hour or more. This leisurely pace forces even the most restless workaholic to relax. While waiting for the tea to brew, you start to focus more intently on your surroundings and notice little details that you would usually rush past without a glance. You might use this time to think about life, reflecting on where you have been and where you are headed. Given the restful pace and lack of distractions, if you drink tea with a friend there is a good chance you will talk about deeper matters than usual. Bringing tea into your life can foster self-cultivation, make you a more peaceful and spiritual person, and deepen your relationships with other people.

Leaves

Tea consumed in the West is usually chopped into a uniform powder or hidden away inside opaque tea-bags. While extremely convenient, this over-processing robs you of the valuable opportunity to observe the whole leaf. Chinese almost always brew tea from whole leaves, and consumers look down on chopped leaves and tea-bags as signs of dubious quality. According to Chinese thinking, any tea seller who does not want to show off beautiful whole leaves probably has something to hide. When tea has been chopped up or hidden inside bags, an unscrupulous merchant could sweep debris off the floor, dump it into a fancy package, and pawn it off on ignorant consumers. Buying whole-leaf tea is the single best way to increase the likelihood of getting a quality product.

Even before you start to brew tea, inspecting the dry leaves yields important clues about what lies ahead. First, you should note the leaf size, which varies considerably. Generally speaking, larger leaves produce stronger and more complex tea. However, complexity isn't always good. As leaves mature on the tree, they lose some of their natural sweetness and begin to develop acrid flavors. The decision of when to harvest has enormous influence on taste. For example, aged *puer* is usually made with large mature leaves, giving it rich, earthy tones overlaid with intriguing complex flavors. In contrast, extremely small young sprouts might produce a weak but exquisitely delicate brew.

Usually a sprout and one to five older leaves are harvested from each twig. Tea experts constantly debate the ideal size and age of leaves for making different kinds of tea, as picking them too young can result in an insipid beverage whereas waiting too long will produce a rough brew. Knowing when to pick the leaves for each kind of tea is vital to the farmer's art, and they agonize over these decisions. A glance at the whole dried leaves reveals their painstaking choices.

The tea tree has been intensively domesticated for centuries. It hybridizes easily, and over time farmers and scientists have developed hundreds of distinctive varieties. Each type of tree has been selectively bred to thrive in a particular area and produces a specific kind of tea. A leaf's shape shows what kind of tree produced it. Some leaves are plump ovals; others are thin and short. Leaves can be either rounded or pointed at the tip. They also vary considerably in thickness, color, and oiliness. If you pay attention to the different kinds of leaves, you will gradually learn which tastes are associated with major hybrids.

A leaf's color is another noticeable attribute, and this is mainly a byproduct of processing. All tea leaves start off green, but processing turns them many different colors. Dried leaves range across a wide spectrum from white and gray, through the many various hues of green, to brown, red, and black. Most importantly, color indicates the degree of oxidation. Light green leaves are either unoxidized or very lightly oxidized, dark green leaves are semi-oxidized, while red, brown, and black leaves are usually fully oxidized. Over time, ageing will eventually turn any tea jet black.

Each kind of tea undergoes a slightly different combination of steps during processing. Even teas in the same general family, such as the various oolongs, can vary considerably in their processing. Common procedures include stirring the leaves in a large wok over a fire, baking them in a charcoal oven, sun drying, machine processing, oxidizing, steaming, crushing, rolling, compressing, and ageing. The way a tea was made determines its final appearance, so examining a dried leaf carefully can reveal a surprising amount of information about how it was processed.

Dry leaves emit a discernable fragrance that usually differs from the smell they produce when infused in hot water, so sniffing dry leaves divulges important information about a tea's characteristics and quality. Most fundamentally, teas of each degree of oxidation emit a distinctive smell. On top of this, each type and grade of tea has its unique aroma. Even with minimal experience it is easy to distinguish the basic style of tea, such as green or red, with just one sniff. Over time it becomes possible to identify different kinds of tea within a particular category, distinguishing between a Taiwan and Fujian oolong just by smelling the leaves. Generally speaking, tea leaves that exude a sweet smell will probably yield an excellent brew. Ageing transforms the characteristics of the leaves, imparting unusual aromas evocative of

Song Dynasty Tea Preparation

camphor, earth, or wood, so most aged tea is easy to identify by smell. Of course, tea that stinks like mud or mold will probably taste terrible, while tea leaves with no smell at all will produce a flavorless brew.

The leaves also reveal how a tea ought to be brewed and how many leaves to put into the pot or cup. Flat leaves will not expand much when wet, so you may need to use a fair number. Most leaves are crinkled during processing to bring more of the inner essences to the surface. Crinkled leaves expand quite a bit as they absorb water, so you do not need to use as many. Gunpowder tea and Taiwanese high-mountain oolongs are tightly rolled into balls, crushing cells in the leaf's interior to squeeze out its inner juices and bring maximum flavor to the surface. Balled tea will expand to surprising dimensions when hot water is added, so relatively few leaves are needed.

Leaf shape also influences taste. Straight leaves release their inner flavors gradually, lending the tea more rhythm as different tastes and aromas slowly emerge in succession. In contrast, crinkled and balled teas discharge their flavors more quickly, giving an intense flavor from the start. Chinese red tea is sometimes chopped into a uniform coarse powder in imitation of tea from India and Sri Lanka. Chopping allows a tea's inner essence to leach out into the water quickly, although this inevitably sacrifices much of the rhythm.

After you finish drinking a pot of good tea, be sure to open the lid and examine the limp moist leaves inside. Tea leaves often change their appearance substantially when wet, and some important details become clear only after the leaves have expanded. The size and shape of many tea leaves only become apparent when wet. Also, the color of dry and wet leaves is always quite different, and connoisseurs routinely use both colors to describe a particular tea. The flexibility and texture of the wet leaves also varies noticeably. For example, certain Fujian oolongs are covered with odd white bumps that only become visible when the leaves are wet. Some leaves become extremely glossy and slippery. Good young tea is soft and flexible when wet. A hard, leathery feel indicates that the tea was made from mature leaves. Aged leaves usually reveal a rough surface and darker color and are somewhat less flexible than fresh tea leaves. Be sure to note the rate of expansion so you can decide how many leaves to use the next time you brew the same tea.

Aroma

Compared to the taste receptors in the mouth, which can make out only a few flavors, the nose is incredibly sensitive. Most of our enjoyment of tea comes from its myriad odors, even if our brain often misinterprets these olfactory sensations as tastes. When tea is in the mouth, sometimes it is difficult to distinguish taste from smell, and we mistakenly assume that the two sensations are a unity when, in fact, we are experiencing them through entirely different senses.

The smell emitted by tea leaves passes through five phases: the aroma of the dry leaves at room temperature; dry leaves when heated; wet leaves steeped in hot water; the intimate aroma emitted by tea in the mouth; and the ethereal smell that clings to the cup after it has been emptied and that also wafts up inside the throat after tea has been swallowed. Each of these aromas is somewhat different.

Many factors affect the aroma of tea. For example, the size of the pot influences a tea's strength and hence its odor, while a teacup's size and shape affect our perception of the smells drifting up from the liquid's surface. Experiment with different tea wares and brewing techniques to learn how these affect aroma and flavor. Armed with this knowledge, you can systematically enhance your tea-drinking experience.

Most good tea has a pleasant, sweet aroma. Inferior leaves are sometimes almost odorless, while spoiled tea can give off a horrible stench. Chinese connoisseurs have come up with some useful technical terms to describe different scents. Most fundamentally, aroma is described in terms of intensity, such as light or heavy. If the smell does not include anything unpleasant and the various component odors do not clash, it is called pure. Tea might also smell burnt, roasted, sun dried, aged, or mildewed, and each of these telltale scents reveals clues about processing and storage.

In fact, the aroma of tea consists of many individual elements, and these differ from cup to cup. Drinkers often describe the components of a tea's fragrance by comparing them to similar odors. Some of the most common similes they use include lotus, orchid, green olive, almond, jujube, sugarcane, glutinous rice, green (*qing*—the vegetable smell of unfermented tea leaves), tangerine, broth, egg yolk, milk, caramel, wood, smoke, camphor, ginseng, mildew, and earth. While these smells might be common in China, some are less frequently encountered elsewhere. Feel free to draw comparisons with a personal palette of familiar smells and use these to build up a practical vocabulary for understanding and describing the components of the aroma emitted by each kind of tea. Of course, most of the smells emitted by tea are unique, and we lack the words to describe them adequately. Experience brings familiarity, however, and veteran drinkers can mentally compare and contrast these nameless smells whenever they sniff a cup of tea.

Flavor

The flavor of tea is produced by the interaction of a multitude of elements. Each tea leaf contains more than 600 chemicals, and these carry numerous flavors that include sweet, sour, bitter, savory, and even a minute amount of salt. The relative proportions of these chemicals determine the overall taste of each cup. This interplay between so many compounds explains why tea has such a complex flavor. Moreover, the taste of tea changes slightly every second as it brews because new chemicals are constantly leaching out into the hot water, as the leaves release some of their interior chemicals faster than others. With each infusion, new flavors come to the forefront. The term *qi* means "spirit" or "vitality," and spirited tea has an intriguingly complex flavor and aroma. Interesting tea is also praised as "lively" (*huo*). A tea is "smooth" (*shunkou*) if the various flavors are well balanced.

Chinese experts point out that we actually taste tea in three different parts of the mouth: on top of the tongue, on the tongue's underside, and along the inside of the cheeks. Each of these spots has a unique set of receptors and nerves, some more sensitive to a specific flavor than others. The different ways that each part of the mouth experiences a sip of tea contribute to our overall sensation of complex flavor. A sophisticated drinker will sometimes take the time to break down the overall flavor into its component physical sensations by noting how it tastes in each part of the mouth.

The most immediately noticeable aspect of a tea's taste is its strength, which goes from strong (*nong*) to weak (*dan*). Strong tea with intensely layered flavors can be praised as "thick" while a weaker tea is "soft." Some teas are naturally stronger than others. Even so, the strength of a particular tea can vary enormously depending upon how it's brewed. Hotter water and a smaller pot invariably yield stronger tea. Strength also varies with each infusion. The first infusion of good tea tends to be very strong, whereas a much weaker brew will be produced the sixth time you add water to the pot. Endurance is another important concept, and this is not the same as strength. Some teas are extremely strong on the first infusion then immediately taper off to become insipid with the second. Good tea leaves usually have superior endurance and can be infused several times.

Between 10% to 20% of the tea leaf consists of various natural sugars, so good tea tastes slightly sweet. It also contains an amino acid called theanine which is both sweet and savory. Chinese distinguish two kinds of sweetness. *Tian* describes a sweetness like refined sugar. Some teas contain tiny amounts of sucrose and similar natural sugars that supply a light natural sweetness. A less familiar kind of sweetness is called *gan*, an extremely useful concept that unfortunately lacks an English equivalent. *Gan* refers to a sensation analogous to sweetness but not at all sugary. The best way to experience *gan* is to swallow a sip of top grade oolong, purse your lips, and inhale quickly through your mouth. You should perceive a lingering flavor that seems sweet but not sugary. *Gan* is always an extremely desirable quality in tea.

Opposite tastes include bitter (*ku*), sour (*suan*), and acrid (*se*). Caffeine is bitter, as are phenolic compounds, and much of a tea's bitterness comes from these chemicals. A few teas lack any trace of overt bitterness, and these are prized for their smoothness. When most teas are brewed to high strength, however, some bitterness is usually noticeable. Bitterness is not necessarily bad. In fact, a bitter note, perceived at the rear of the tongue, is crucial to the well-balanced taste of many famous teas. More than a thousand years ago, Chinese tea experts identified the intriguing interplay between sweet and bitter as the key to great tea. Although novice tea-drinkers might find any trace of bitterness unpleasant, connoisseurs consider a slightly bitter undertaste a desirable counterbalance to strong sweetness and floral fragrance—much like the classic Western pairing of bitter chocolate and sweet processed sugar. A tea devoid of bitterness has to compensate with extraordinary flavor or else it will just come off as watery and uninteresting.

Sourness is present to some degree in most oxidized or aged teas. We sense sour flavors on the central surface of the tongue. This is another flavor that can be either good or bad, depending upon how it interacts with other tastes. If acidity is one note in a symphony of flavors, it can be interesting and positive. Many great teas have a slight sour tinge. But when sourness is singular and overwhelming, the result is dreadful. Sometimes an unpleasantly sour tea can be salvaged by reducing water temperature or shortening steeping time. Either method will decrease the amount of acid that leaches out into the water.

Although acridness might not sound particularly nice, it is not necessarily a negative trait. This taste comes mainly from astringent phenolic compounds in the leaf. Of course, tea that has been ineptly processed or made from inferior plants might have a disgustingly strong acrid flavor. Stems usually have an acrid taste, so tea becomes unpleasant when too many stems are mixed in with the leaves. For this reason, good tea usually has relatively few stems. However, sometimes a touch of acridity can lend a tea more rhythm and character. Fine Fujian cliff teas such as white cockscomb, for example, feature acridness as one stroke in a varied palette of flavors, and many meticulously processed premium Taiwan oolongs deliberately include some stems along with the leaves to give the final flavor more interest. Some people believe that leaves taste best when dried over charcoal because a tiny amount of smoke makes its way into tea, giving the flavor some challenging complexity. Oxidation usually smoothes over a tea's rough edges, so excessive acridity is most likely to be problem in low grade green tea. Steeping leaves in very hot water will increase acrid flavors, which explains why green tea is brewed at a relatively low temperature.

Most people don't know that tea can be brewed with cold water. In fact, this is the best way to make iced tea. The advantage to cold brewing is that very few acrid or bitter flavors emerge, producing an exceptionally smooth beverage. The color is also clearer than hot-brewed iced tea, which can turn cloudy when ice is added. To make tea this way, just stir some leaves into room temperature water in a ceramic bowl, cover it with plastic wrap, and let it stand for up to twenty-four hours. You can also let the tea steep in the refrigerator, in which case it will already be cold as soon as it is ready.

Ageing imparts unique odors and flavors. This process deliberately invites various benign microbes, mold, and fungi to grow on dry leaves during storage. Because ageing is carried out by so many different fermentation agents, the results are extremely varied and difficult to predict. Chinese describe the taste that results from ageing very generally as *chen* or *shou*. However, these vague terms are misnomers, as ageing is not a single taste but rather a complex process that generates a wide range of new flavors. Some aged tea develops a strong camphor taste and smell while others have a musty aroma but very smooth flavor. Sometimes ageing intensifies flavor to hair-raising extremes, while in other teas the taste almost completely disappears over time.

The taste of bad tea can suffer from a range of defects. Some are extremely watery and have virtually no taste at all. An absence of flavor is usually due to inferior leaves or improper processing. Other substandard teas have the opposite problem and suffer from smelly odors and flavors such as mud or earth. Some aged *puer* has a pleasant light mildew taste that may not universally understood but which its fans consider desirable. More commonly, however, mildew is a sign of improper storage. It grows rapidly when unsealed tea is stored in a warm, humid place without proper ventilation. Finally, there are teas that lack any specifically bad flavors, yet the tastes do not blend together into a pleasingly balanced whole so the overall impression is unappealing.

At first glance, the term rhythm (*yun*) might seem extremely mysterious, but, in fact, this concept is absolutely essential for understanding good tea. The taste and smell of tea is not static as it brews in the pot. Chemical compounds leach out of the leaves at different rates, creating a constantly shifting series of sensations in the nose and mouth. A tea with rhythm has a complex and intriguing progression of flavors and aromas that give the drinker a lively experience. Rhythm is the key to great tea, and this is what makes tea so much more interesting than other beverages. For example, rhythm is the most basic difference between tea and coffee. Tea changes continuously while it brews whereas a pot of coffee just sits there, completely static. Once you become attuned to the intricate drama constantly unfolding in a steeping pot of tea, other drinks seem lifeless in comparison.

Rhythm also explains why written descriptions of tea sometimes seem so inadequate. You might read about a particular tea smelling like orchids or tasting like tangerine, then be disappointed when you don't find these characteristics in the first cup that comes out of the pot. Remember that the flavor of tea unfolds in a long, gradual sequence that changes from minute to minute. Oftentimes a particular flavor will only be present for one phase of a tea's development. Proceeding and successive flavors might be quite different.

'Throat" (*houlong*) is another very useful concept, and this quality is present in almost every great tea. Chinese experts divide taste into two general categories: the flavor of tea in the mouth, and the lingering taste experienced after the liquid has been swallowed. The latter flavor is called "throat," and this is often very different from mouth flavor. Although throat is usually thought of as a kind of taste, in fact, the main sensation is caused by fumes that waft up into the nose from the drinker's throat, so it is actually more a smell than a taste. Sweet throat is always the best. Other terms to describe throat include rich, strong, weak, dry, sandy, prickly, and chilly.

Song Dynasty Jian Ware Bowl

Throat can be simulated by sniffing a cup after it has been emptied, a smell called cold aroma. The sweet smell that gathers in the emptied cup parallels what happens in the throat after tea is swallowed, which is why Chinese drinkers sometimes use tall sniffing cups in addition to squat drinking cups. Interestingly, cold aroma usually changes remarkably over the course of about a minute, and it often intensifies considerably before fading out. You should smell the sniffing cup several times to note how the cold aroma develops, as this is an excellent guide to how the tea will act in the throat.

Color

A tea's color is produced by the reflection of light off the liquid. Of course, the type of light has considerable influence on the color we perceive. Few people would ever stop to think how different kinds of light affect tea color, but proper lighting is essential for distinguishing a tea's true color. Florescent lighting is especially bad because it gives any liquid a lurid green tint. Of course, natural light is best, but a warm bulb that mimics sunlight is a good substitute.

Tea ware also influences color. The deeper the cup, the darker the color will be. A shallow cup will always display color more clearly. Also, the cup's interior serves as the tea's background, so if the cup has a dark lining you will not be able to make out the tea's real color. A teacup with a light interior is obviously preferable, and

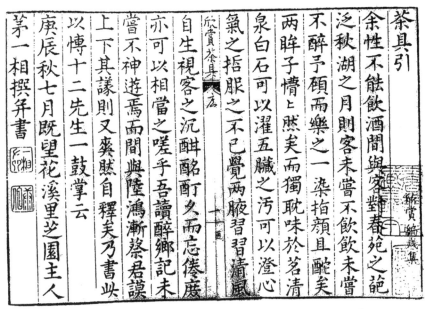

Xinshang Chaju—A Ming Dynasty Book on Tea Ware Appreciation

white is best of all. For this reason, even cups made of dark Yixing clay are often lined with white porcelain. In recent years, some drinkers have even begun using little glass teapots. Although these obviously are not traditional, a glass container gives drinkers the best idea of the tea's true color. The way tea is brewed can also influence its color quite a bit. The number of leaves in the pot, water temperature, and steeping time all have a major impact.

Color is an inescapable feature of tea appreciation. The most basic classification of Chinese tea (as white, green, yellow, oolong, red, and black) is based mostly on the color of the liquid. With some experience, it is possible to identify a tea's general type just by looking at its color. Veteran drinkers can also use color to judge how strongly a tea has been brewed and whether or not it has reached proper strength. If a tea is unusually dark or light for its type, you know that something has probably gone wrong. Pale tea might mean that you used too few leaves or insufficiently hot water whereas an unexpectedly dark color might indicate the opposite problem. The tint can also reveal overall quality. Pure, clean, bright shades usually indicate good tea; a murky tinge will alert you that something is amiss.

Density

The density of tea varies according to the amount of natural oil. The tea tree contains quite a bit of oil, and tea seeds are even pressed to extract an aromatic cooking-oil. Tea oil is a fragrant substitute for sesame oil, which it resembles in color and taste. Although most of the tea tree's oil is concentrated in its seeds, the leaves contain a little oil as well. The amount of oil in a pot of tea might be miniscule, but it nevertheless has a major impact on taste and mouth feel. Tea oil is the vehicle for a wide range of flavors, some of them quite subtle. For this reason, leaves are sometimes crushed, chopped, or rolled into balls to bring more oil to the surface. Oil is also the ideal medium for conveying tastes and odors, which is why fragrant substances are processed into essential oils to make them usable as flavorings. If tea were not slightly oily, it would not be nearly as fragrant and tasty. So the amount of oil in a particular kind of tea has a subtle influence on its aroma as well as physical texture.

Oil makes the liquid heavier than plain warm water, and the degree of density differs from one tea to the next. A tea can be generally described as thick or thin, depending upon the amount of tea oil and other dense chemical compounds relative to the surrounding water. The texture of thin teas is little different from pure water, and these usually have a light flavor. Thick tea results when the leaves release more oily chemicals into the water, making the liquid richer in texture and also giving it a more intense flavor. When the level of tea oil is high enough, particles of tea are held in suspension. In a very thick tea you can observe tiny flecks of leaf that hover in the middle of the liquid rather than sinking to the bottom.

Veteran tea-drinkers use many other terms besides thick and thin to describe density. This specialized jargon includes words such as slippery, sandy, soft, hard, sharp, gentle, lively, and changeable. Most of these concepts are extremely abstract and metaphorical, and their meaning can only be grasped with experience. If you pay close attention to the sensation of the liquid in your mouth, these enigmatic terms will begin to make sense.

Water

Although we usually think of water as completely neutral in flavor, in fact, each source has a distinct taste. Good water is one of the primary flavors in the cup, and tea made with distilled water seems strangely insipid. Because water provides the background flavor of tea, the great authorities of the past always stressed its importance. They believed that water from certain places improves flavor, and particular wells and streams became famous as sources of the best tea water. In imperial times, most water was less than pristine, so water purity was a major problem facing tea-drinkers. The Tang dynasty expert Lu Yu even recommended straining tea water through a metal filter to remove polluting particles. This advice gives us an idea of what most people's drinking water must have been like a thousand years ago. Even today, water quality in China can be extremely uncertain, and the purity of tap water is not always assured. Of course, if water is polluted or has an odd taste, it is unsuitable for making tea.

Fortunately, nowadays good clean water is readily available in developed countries. If the tap water where you live is not sufficiently neutral in flavor, you should brew tea from bottled still water. Water for tea should be extremely pure and not too alkaline, with a pH around 7.0, as the flavor and texture of hard water are inappropriate for tea. Tea leaves are somewhat acid, so the resulting liquid should have a pH of about 5.5. Strongly flavored water should be avoided. Of course, tea water should not have any odd tastes from minerals such as iron, magnesium, or calcium, nor should it have any trace of mud, organic decay, or chemical stench.

Part II

Famous Chinese Teas

Chapter 5

White Tea

While most tea leaves are processed by heating with fire or electricity, white tea dries out naturally under the sun, giving it a unique appearance and flavor. White tea is named after its light colored, young leaves, which range in hue from pure white to silver and muted green. The delicate pale liquid is fragrant, sweet, and low in caffeine. A so-called white tea was produced during the Tang and Song dynasties, but this seems to have been a regular green tea with a high proportion of white young leaves. Modern sun-dried white tea dates back to about the mid-sixteenth century.

The light flavor of white tea is well suited for hot summer days, while the low caffeine level makes it the best choice when you feel like drinking tea in the evening. It can be brewed in a covered cup or a small pot. Because white tea is so light, you need to use more leaves than usual. The leaves will release unpleasant flavors if they get too hot, so water about 75°–80° C (165°–175° F) is standard. While the leaves are steeping, they float to the surface and then slowly sink. Unlike most tea, the leaves contract in size when brewed.

Because the water temperature is so low and flavor so weak, white tea takes a long time to brew, ten minutes being usual. As it starts to steep, the liquid is a very light green. The tea slowly deepens in hue to become pale yellow, at which point it is ready. Another way to judge brewing time is by observing the leaves. When about half the leaves have sunk to the bottom of the vessel, the tea should be ready, although lower quality leaves might need more time to brew. White tea is best prepared in a white covered cup or small glass teapot, both of which allow you observe the true color of the liquid and to keep track of what is happening to the leaves. Premium leaves (such as silver needle white down) can be infused twice, although lesser white tea (like white peony) is usually good for only one slow infusion.

Silver Needle White Down (*yinzhen baohao*) 銀針白毫

The finest white tea is officially named silver needle white down, but many people call it just silver needle or white down for short. Sometimes the name is inverted as white down silver needle. This tea is made entirely from tender young sprouts. As the leaves dry in the sun, they curl inward along their length and end up as uniform greenish-white or gray cylinders. The furry leaves are sharply pointed on both ends, hence the name silver needle. A tea called silver needle was produced during the Song dynasty, but it was probably quite different from the modern version. Modern white tea by this name seems to have been produced during the Ming dynasty. The current

Silver Needle White Down

version was first grown in Fuding County, Fujian. During the late nineteenth century, farmers in neighboring Zhenghe County also started raising silver needle. An unusual hybrid grown in the area produces dainty sprouts appropriate for white tea.

The leaves are harvested in spring, when the young sprouts are largest and have the finest flavor. Processing is extremely simple. Unlike most teas, silver needle is neither crushed nor rolled. The leaves are simply spread across large bamboo trays and set out in the sun to dry. If the weather is unusually hot, drying is done entirely under the sun. Tea processed in this way is called *maozhen* (hairy needles). But since most leaves are harvested at springtime, the weather is usually not hot enough to dry them out completely with sunlight alone. Typically the leaves are exposed to sunlight until 80–90% of the moisture has evaporated, then drying is completed over a very low fire at little more than room temperature. These tender sprouts produce an exceptionally smooth, delicate tea with a fine fragrance, honeyed sweetness, and a hint of tangerine. Although not everyone appreciates its ethereal flavor, some consider silver needle the epitome of sophisticated refinement.

White Peony (*bai mudan*) 白牡丹 白牡丹

This tea's poetic name is inspired by the eccentric contours the leaves assume during drying, when they twist into irregular shapes said to resemble small flowers. Nowadays the leaves are sometimes tied up with string to form little artificial flowers, making them look even more like their namesake. This variety of tea was invented in 1922 in Jian'ou County, Fujian and is now produced in several nearby counties (Jianyang, Zhenghe, Songxi, Fuding, and elsewhere). It comes from a tree similar to the silver needle hybrid, so white peony is basically a lower grade version of silver needle white down. An intermediate grade in-between regular white peony and silver needle is marketed as white peony king. Because white peony is made from older leaves, it usually costs only about a fifth as much as silver needle, although of course it never tastes as good.

This tea is produced only from leaves picked in spring. One sprout and two young leaves, often covered with fine down, are harvested from each stem. These are spread out on bamboo trays and dried indoors until 95% of the internal moisture has evaporated. Final drying is done over a fire, but at a temperature much higher than that used to finish off silver needle. As they dry, some leaves contract into cylinders while others remain flat, and they end up as an unusually diverse range of shapes and sizes. Colors also vary considerably and include white, gray, silver, and light green. The pale yellow liquid is slightly sweet and, in better grades, includes a hint of plum or peach flavor. Unlike silver needle, which is completely smooth, white peony is sometimes slightly acrid.

Shoumei 壽眉

The third and most common type of white tea is variously known as *shoumei* (old man's eyebrows), *gongmei* (tribute eyebrows), or *xiaobai* (little white). Western tea merchants sometimes use *shoumei* as a generic name for all white tea. In China, *gongmei* can also refer to premium *shoumei*. Whatever you call it, this tea comes from a different hybrid than that for silver needle white down and white peony, and thus has a distinct flavor. *Shoumei* is mostly grown in Jianyang County, Fujian,

Shoumei

although nearby Jianou and Pucheng Counties also produce some as well.

Processing is the same as for white peony. There are many grades and varieties of *shoumei*, and prices vary considerably. This tea consists of a jumble of sprouts and older leaves. The older leaves are naturally crinkled and have a greenish tint while the sprouts tend to be white. Some people claim that *shoumei* tastes best if slowly infused in relatively cool water, although another school of thought contends that *shoumei* is fundamentally different from other white teas and should be brewed at a relatively high temperature between 90°–100° C (195°–210° F). *Shoumei* produces a fragrant yellow liquid that is slightly sweet and sometimes carries a hint of plum flavor, although it can be slightly acrid.

Chapter 6

Green Tea

When Chinese people talk about green tea they can mean one of two very different things. In popular usage, "green tea" is as vague in Chinese as in English and refers loosely to any unoxidized or lightly oxidized tea, including a wide spectrum of what would be more strictly classified as white, green, yellow, and oolong teas. In technical jargon, however, green refers specifically to tea that has been heated in a wok or oven (unlike white tea, which is sun dried) but has not been oxidized (unlike yellow or oolong tea). Because processing is minimal, green tea retains much of the chlorophyll and other natural vegetable flavors of the leaf and often tastes somewhat like spinach, seaweed, or green olive. This is the most ancient kind of tea, and until the last few centuries all tea was green.

The processing method for green tea is straightforward. First, the leaves are heated over a fire or in an oven to evaporate some internal moisture. Next, they may be crushed or twisted to bring some tea oil to the surface, although some green teas (such as the famous *longjing*) have straight leaves. They are then heated again to finish drying. During processing, the leaves are sometimes left to sit awhile to dry out or cool down, but never long enough for oxidation to begin.

Because green tea is easy to make and refreshing to drink, it is grown over a vast area. One Chinese book dedicated to green tea lists 132 varieties, while a respected Chinese tea encyclopedia includes 138 kinds, but many of the teas they describe are different. In addition, I have personally tasted a number of other green teas and heard of even more that do not appear in either of these detailed reference works. The number of green teas is clearly large, probably in the hundreds. Most are grown and consumed locally and never reach a wide market. Not all of these humble local teas deserve their obscurity, and it is not difficult to uncover some excellent regional green teas completely unknown to even the most experienced connoisseurs in Shanghai or Beijing.

Because processing is minimal, green teas are extremely delicate and highly susceptible to damage by humidity or sunlight. They can go bad quickly if not properly stored in a tightly sealed container and kept in a dark place. Some people even put green tea in the refrigerator to keep it fresh. If you opt for this method, make sure the container is perfectly sealed so the tea does not pick up any odd tastes like blue cheese or onions. I consider the dangers of refrigeration to outweigh the benefits, and I keep my tea in airtight containers in a cabinet at room temperature. Buying green tea in small amounts is the best way to guarantee freshness and avoid storage problems.

Although green tea tastes bright and fresh, the lack of oxidation has a major drawback. Oxidation tends to cover up or ameliorate certain unpleasant tastes, so green tea usually carries some disagreeable trace flavors. In a large Western teapot, green leaves will produce little more than lightly flavored water, whereas a small Yixing teapot intensifies the brew to the point that unpleasant bitter and acrid flavors come to the forefront. To overcome these problems, most drinkers brew green tea in a covered cup rather than a teapot.

Because green tea is brewed and consumed in the same cup, it is the most convenient type of tea to drink. Just scoop out enough leaves to cover the bottom of a covered cup, pour on hot water, replace the lid, and let it steep until ready. Do not use too many leaves or let them sit too long or else the tea will become objectionably acrid. Because green tea is unoxidized, it is especially rich in astringent phenolic compounds that can be unpleasant if too strong. Water temperature is also important, as very hot water will extract unwanted tastes from the leaves. Relatively cool water, about 70°–85° C (160°–185° F), is optimal. Besides traditional hot tea, green iced tea is the world's most refreshing drink for hot summer days. Green tea is an excellent match for seafood, and teas with a strong seaweed flavor, such as *longjing*, are the perfect accompaniment for sashimi.

Since green teas are so numerous, a comprehensive overview is impossible here. What follows are descriptions of a few of the best and most representative green teas. A resourceful tea buff traveling through China can easily track down a profusion of interesting green teas not listed here. Good green tea has a bright refreshing taste that makes it extremely drinkable and easy to appreciate. Anyone with a curious palate will enjoy exploring China's rich trove of green teas, few of which are known abroad.

Longjing (**Dragon Well,** *lung ching*) 龍井

Longjing (literally, "dragon well") is the name of a town near Hangzhou and scenic West Lake in Jiangsu where farmers have been growing fine tea since the Tang dynasty. The name *longjing* is now applied to all green tea grown in the general area. According to legend, tea was first introduced there by a Buddhist monk who transplanted tea trees from the

Longjing

famous Tiantai Temple, and eighteen ancient trees in the Shifeng area continue to yield this old style tea. *Longjing* was an article of imperial tribute during the Song and Qing dynasties, and today it is widely considered the world's finest green tea.

The *longjing* region near West Lake is divided into several smaller areas. Each has a somewhat different terrain, climate, and soil and so produces distinctive tea. Important *longjing* appellations include Shifeng, Meijiawu, Baihe, Tianzhu, Yunqi, Hupao, and Longjing town proper. Four shorthand names are sometimes used for the main regional varieties: lion (*shi*—from Shifeng), dragon (*long*—after Longjing town), cloud (*yun*—Yunqi and Meijiawu, the largest area of production), and tiger (*hu*—Hupao). Another common system divides *longjing* into three general grades: Shifeng, Meiwu, and West Lake.

The quality of *longjing* tea varies enormously, ranging from sublime to dreadful. In 1995, the Chinese government standardized the grading system for *longjing* and now it is officially classified into fourteen grades of quality. Premium tea from the Shifeng area is considered the finest. In addition, farmers in other parts of mainland China and Taiwan produce green teas in a similar style and market them as *longjing*.

Longjing comes from several kinds of tea tree, including so-called long leaf, round leaf, melon leaf, Pingyang early tea, and a superior new variety called *longjing* No. 43. Of course each hybrid produces somewhat different tea. *Longjing* leaves look like dried grass. They are usually straight and fairly uniform in higher grades, but sometimes the sides curl inward. Each leaf is usually pale green, edged with yellow, and has a brown central vein running down the middle. Leaves from Shifeng often have an unusual yellow tinge, and even when fresh they can emit a funky odor reminiscent of aged leaves.

71

The time of harvest has a major influence on the characteristics of each batch, so tea picked in spring can taste very different from autumn tea taken from the same tree. Generally speaking, the earlier in the season the tea is picked the better. The first flush of spring is best, followed by a late spring flush, an early summer harvest, and finally autumn tea. The best grade consists entirely of unopened leaf buds called dragon sprouts or water lily hearts that are harvested in the first flush. Next in quality comes sparrow tongue tea harvested later in the spring or early summer. This is made from one sprout and one new leaf, with the sprout longer than the leaf. According to jargon that dates back a thousand years, a sprout is called a "spear" (*qiang*) and the first leaf a "banner" (*qi*). West Lake farmers call middle grade *longjing* either "banner spear" (one sprout and one leaf) or "brown rice banner spear" (one opened sprout and one or two leaves).

Processing is simple. After harvest the leaves are spread out to dry indoors for 8–10 hours, during which they lose 15–20% of their weight. This initial air drying intensifies flavor and decreases acridity. Next, the leaves are carefully stirred by hand in a hot wok using a special motion to give them their characteristic flat shape, then spread out to cool for an hour. Finally, the leaves are returned to the wok to finish drying. Some teashops in Hangzhou will process the leaves while you wait so you can enjoy the spectacle of watching them being hand stirred in the wok, then go home with a bag of immaculately fresh tea.

Some connoisseurs brew this tea in a glass because the leaves are so attractive. Optimal water temperature is on the high side for green teas, about 85° C (185° F), and there are iconoclasts who say that the water should be close to boiling. The resulting liquid is a shade of yellow described as the color of brown rice. *Longjing* has an unusually strong flavor for green tea, redolent with assertive tastes such as grass, spinach, or seaweed. In addition to the predominant vegetable flavor, good *longjing* features a complex interplay of extremely varied and sometimes surprising scents. For example, some tea from Shifeng has subtle aromas of orchid, egg yolk, and broth. Meijiawu *longjing* carries strong floral scents, while tea from nearby Baihe can hint at egg yolk and curry. This intriguing range of smells and tastes promises great rewards to the *longjing* fan.

Huangshan Furry Peak (Huangshan *maofeng*) 黃山毛峰

Huangshan is one the most beautiful mountain ranges in China, and its twisted trees and jagged rocks have inspired painters for centuries. The high altitude and misty weather also make it an ideal place to grow tea. Farmers have been raising tea on the mountain since the Song dynasty, and Huangshan green tea became famous during the Ming era. Although these gorgeous peaks have recently been desecrated by an explosion of tacky tourist facilities, the area continues to produce superb green tea.

Huangshan Furry Peak

The current variety of tea dates back only to the late nineteenth century and descends from a natural hybrid discovered growing near a local temple. At first this exceptional tea was called "Huangshan clouds and mist" or just "Huangshan cloud" for short. A savvy merchant realized its commercial potential and convinced local farmers to raise quality by adopting better production methods. The marriage of a superior hybrid with meticulous processing gave birth to one of world's great teas, ultimately known as Huangshan furry peak.

This tea comes in four grades, classed mainly according to the age of the leaves at harvest. Superior tea consists of one sprout and one young leaf, both covered with the trademark furry down. The next three grades are made from two or three older leaves along with a sprout from each twig. There are also two special superior types called golden flakes (*jinhuang pian*) and ivory-colored (*xiangya se*) furry peak, which taste somewhat different from the standard variety. To maintain freshness, this tea is always processed on the day of harvest. The leaves are heated in a wok to reduce water content, rolled to twist them, and then baked until completely dry.

This tea is described as furry because the sprouts are covered with down, and they are compared to peaks because each leaf comes to a sharp point at the end. Overall, the yellowish green leaves are thin and slightly curled, an unusual shape often compared to the tongue of a swallow. The leaves range in color from old ivory to golden yellow and produce a beautifully fragrant liquid with an unusually strong flavor for green tea. The rich sweet taste is topped off with a faint smokiness and ends in an extremely sweet throat. The top grade of furry peak is incredibly smooth and lacks any of the trace bitterness and acridity of commonplace green tea. The premium version also has superb endurance and maintains its flavor for several infusions.

Dongting Biluo spring (Dongting Biluo *chun*) 洞庭碧螺春

Dongting is a mountain range near Lake Taihu in Wu County, Jiangsu. One of the peaks there is called Biluo. The word *chun* means "spring," which is when this tea is harvested. It so happens that the Chinese characters for Biluo can also be read as "green spiral seashells," and this poetic name is said to describe the twisted shape of the green leaves perfectly. The Dongting Mountains are covered with fruit orchards, and tea fields are interspersed among flowering apricot, persimmon, pomegranate, and peach trees, creating one of China's most beautiful agricultural landscapes. The tea is said to absorb scents from the surrounding fruits, lending it unusual complexity.

Tea has been grown in the Dongting area since the Tang dynasty. Dongting Biluo spring has been produced since at least the Ming dynasty, and by the early Qing period it was designated an imperial tribute tea. Today it is universally considered one of China's greatest teas. In addition to the authentic article, a small amount of good quality imitation Biluo spring is produced near Sanxia in Taipei County, Taiwan.

One sprout and one leaf are usually harvested from each twig, and smaller leaves are covered with fine down. Leaves picked early in the season are classed as "spring" flush, while those taken later are "valley rains" flush. The leaves are processed immediately. They are heated in a very hot wok, twisted, and finally baked at low heat to finish drying.

Dongting Biluo spring is divided into seven grades. The leaves are quite small, twisted into tiny beautiful curls, and range in color from silver to green. Many people like to brew this tea in a glass to enjoy the spectacle produced by the unfolding leaves as they bend and turn, a process that has been compared to "rolling clouds and dancing snowflakes." This tea is highly regarded for its strong sweet aroma, which is topped off with a slight floral scent that is long-lasting. The pale green liquid has a rich sweet flavor overlaid with an ethereal peach taste and finishes with excellent throat.

Guzhu Purple Shoot (Guzhu *zisun*) 顧渚紫笋

This tea is grown on Mount Guzhu in Changxing County, Zhejiang. Although the standard name today is Guzhu purple shoot, sometimes it's still called Huzhou purple shoot (Huzhou *zisun*) after an old name for the area. Tang poets praised purple shoot tea, and it was an item of imperial tribute for more than 600 years up through the Ming dynasty. In 770, a special office was even established in Huzhou to produce the emperor's purple shoot tea. Large amounts were produced during the Tang dynasty, and 30,000 people were said to have been involved in the harvest every spring. During the Tang and Song dynasties, purple shoot tea was compressed into disks, but from the Ming dynasty onward loose-leaf tea has been standard. After the Ming era the reputation of purple shoot steadily declined, and by the 1940s most of the former tea fields had been abandoned. Considering the former fame of the tea produced there, it was clear to everyone that the area was well suited for the crop, and production resumed during the late 1970s.

Purple shoot tea consists of one sprout and one young leaf. During processing the leaves sit for five or six hours at room temperature to allow some moisture to evaporate naturally, then they are heated twice in a wok and baked in an oven until completely dry. These leaves produce a pale green liquid that is aromatic, sweet, and carries a fresh taste, finishing off with good throat.

Gunpowder Tea (Pingshui Pearls, Pingshui *zhucha*) 平水珠茶

The technique of rolling tea leaves into tight tiny balls originated in a dozen or so counties around the town of Pingshui in Zhejiang. Tea grown in that part of Zhejiang has traditionally been processed and marketed through Pingshui, so the name of the town is attached to all the tea grown in the general region. Pingshui has been a major tea-growing region since the Tang dynasty, and by the Song period it was famous for a strongly flavored green tea. During the late Qing dynasty most of the local harvest was being sold to foreign merchants, probably because Pingshui is so close to the coast. Because Pingshui's product has been exported for several centuries, tea from this area has had a major impact on Western perceptions of green tea.

In Chinese, balled tea is called "pearl tea" or "round tea." English merchants nicknamed it gunpowder tea because the rolled leaves were said to resemble round musket balls. Chinese find this English name extremely strange and ugly, although this does not keep them from marketing rolled tea as "gunpowder" to appeal to the lucrative Western market. Of course, any tea leaf can be formed into a ball, and rolled tea is produced here and there throughout China. In English, "gunpowder" is often used as a generic term for any balled tea. Pingshui leaves stand out from most other balled teas because of their astonishingly small size. The leaves are fairly small to begin with, and after being tightly rolled the resulting sphere is remarkably dainty and attractive.

The leaves are heated in a wok several times, much the same as green tea elsewhere. As a final step, however, each dark green tea leaf is squeezed and rolled to produce a tiny ball. Because hand-rolling is so labor intensive, this tea was traditionally more expensive than comparable green teas, and its high price gave gunpowder tea a luxurious reputation in the West. In recent years machinery has been introduced to do the rolling, so Pingshui tea is now fairly inexpensive.

The flavor of gunpowder tea is similar to that of other strong green teas except that the tight rolling brings more tea oil to the surface, so the flavors rush out very quickly and produce an intense liquid with little rhythm. Because gunpowder tea is stronger than ordinary green tea, fewer leaves should be used. This tea should also be brewed at a higher temperature than usual, between 90°–100° C (195°–210° F) being optimal.

Taiping Monkey Leader (Taiping *houkui*) 太平猴魁

Several highly regarded and fairly similar greens have been grown in the area around Taiping and Jing Counties in Anhui Province since at least the Ming dynasty. Nowadays the ordinary grade is called "pointed" tea (*jian cha*) while premium varieties include yellow flower cloud points (*huanghua yunjia*n) and Jing County special points (Jing *xian tejian*). The most famous of the premium "pointed" teas is grown on the steep walls of a valley wedged among the scenic Huangshan Mountains.

Taiping Monkey Leader

This tea is called Taiping *houkui*, which literally means Taiping monkey leader. The name of this tea sounds as odd in Chinese as in English and requires explanation. Monkey refers to a place called Monkey Valley (Houkeng) where a nineteenth-century farmer named Wang Kuicheng invented this premium tea by using more refined processing techniques. Taiping is the name of a pond in Monkey Valley. Finally, the term "leader" is from the character *kui* in Wang Kuicheng's given name. In other words, this tea is named after the person who invented it and the place where he lived.

The Taiping monkey leader hybrid has large leaves that are covered with copious white down when young. The tea is made from one sprout and two or three tender young leaves picked in spring. The leaves are quickly heated in a hot wok for 2–3 minutes then baked in an oven three times at progressively lower temperatures. Repeated slow baking is an extremely gentle processing method that gives the tea an unusually subtle flavor. The dried leaves remain straight and flat, come to a sharp point at the tip, and have a central vein described as a "red silk thread." They resemble *longjing* leaves in shape, but the color is much darker.

Monkey Valley is a small place, so little authentic Taiping monkey leader is produced. Inevitably, farmers nearby grow similar tea and market it as monkey leader. Tea from the Taiping area has twelve grades. Premium tea is true monkey leader and makes up the top three grades. Medium quality tea, called "leader points," also consists of three grades. The most ordinary leaves are called "pointed" tea, divided into six grades.

The liquid of top quality authentic Taiping monkey leader is pale green, sweet, relatively weak, and highly aromatic. Monkey leader is particularly famous for its extraordinary rhythm—the flavors and aromas constantly develop as the leaves infuse, so it is almost like drinking several different teas in one sitting. Despite their delicacy, the leaves also have exceptional endurance for green tea and should be good for four infusions.

Liuan Melon Pieces (Liuan *guapian*) 六安瓜片

Liuan in Anhui is home to several well-known teas. The area has produced notable tea since the Song dynasty, and during the Ming and Qing dynasties it was a source of imperial tribute tea. Melon pieces, a modern premium variety, dates back only to the early years of the twentieth century, when local farmers decided to improve quality by using only young tender leaves from the spring flush to produce a special high grade green tea. They originally called this tea melon seed pieces, but the name was soon shortened to melon pieces. Due to its exceptional quality, melon pieces quickly became one of the most highly regarded green teas.

Today this tea is grown along a series of mountains running across Liuan, Jinzhai, and Huoshan Counties. Most comes from Liuan County, although the leaves from Jinzhai are considered the best. Melon pieces are classified into two general types based on region: inner mountain, and outer mountain. Outer mountain melon pieces are grown around Liuan municipality. Tea from Jinzhai, Huoshan, and elsewhere in Liuan County is classified as inner mountain melon pieces. The highest grade is grown on an evergreen-covered Qitoushan Mountain (sometimes called Qishan for short) and marketed under the name Qishan famous pieces (Qishan *mingpian*). Qitoushan is pocketed with caves that are home to enormous numbers of bats. The local farmers fertilize their trees with rich bat guano, giving the plump leaves an intense sweet flavor.

Melon pieces are divided into eight grades according to quality. Qishan famous pieces constitute Grades 1–3. Below this are inner and outer mountain melon pieces, which make up Grades 4–8. Sometimes this tea is classified according to when in the spring it was harvested. The earliest tea is called "carried" tea, then comes melon, and finally plum tea.

The leaves are processed in five steps. After being heated in a hot wok to burn off initial moisture, they are baked four times in a charcoal-heated oven. The gentle drying of repeated baking and cooling gives this tea an unusually delicate flavor while preserving considerable strength. This tea's name implies that the leaves ought to be shaped like a slice of melon or flat melon seed, and maybe this is how they originally looked, but today the name is a misnomer. In fact, the edges curl inward toward the middle and the whole leaf is slightly twisted. They are dark green with a trace of yellow and some white down.

In addition to the usual spinach flavor common to most green teas, melon pieces also carry strong sweet and bitter notes together with a seaweed taste, lending it considerable complexity. The highest grades are superb and yield a sweet fragrant liquid with excellent throat. This tea ages well, developing an extremely intense flavor over time. Sometimes the leaves are wrapped in bamboo leaves and left to ferment for several years or even decades before drinking. Some believe that this tea has special medicinal qualities.

Green Peony (*lü mudan*) 綠牡丹

This tea was produced during the sixteenth century then inexplicably died out. It was revived in the 1980s and is now fairly popular because of its novelty value. Green peony was invented in Jiangshan in Zhejiang Province, although now tea by the same name is made elsewhere. The green liquid has a fairly heavy flavor, but this tea is far more notable for its beautifully shaped leaves than its taste. The uniform leaves are long and thin, and farmers pick a sprout and one or two leaves from each plant. After drying is complete, workers patiently tie together dozens of leaves by wrapping a thin piece of twine around one end, producing a clump of leaves that resembles a flower. When steeped in water, the leaves expand to form petal-like shapes, creating a whimsical floral illusion. Because of its fanciful shape, green peony is almost always brewed in a glass or transparent covered cup. It is sometimes served at banquets as a festive flourish.

Chapter 7

Yellow Tea

Yellow tea has been produced since the late sixteenth century. Because the leaves undergo some gentle oxidation, they yield a pale yellow liquid that gives this tea its name. Yellow teas vary considerably, mostly due to different degrees of oxidation. Some varieties oxidize for less than an hour and are little different from green tea, while others are allowed to sit for more than a week and end up only slightly lighter than a delicate oolong.

Yellow teas come in various grades, and a glance at the size of the leaves usually reveals the general quality. Premium yellow tea is made from sprouts only, giving it an extremely delicate flavor. Ordinary grades consist of a combination of sprouts and leaves, whereas the lowliest teas are mostly mature leaves. Yellow tea can be brewed in a covered cup or a small pot. The water should be relatively cool, approximately 75°–80° C (165°–175° F), to keep unwanted acrid flavors from leaching out.

Junshan Silver Needle (Junshan *yinzhen*) 君山銀針

The most famous yellow tea comes from Junshan, a celebrated mountain shrouded in legend and celebrated in poetry. This peak sits on Qingluo Island amidst picturesque Dongting Lake in Hunan. Tea has been grown in the area since the Tang dynasty, and Qing connoisseurs held Junshan tea in high regard. It was an article of imperial tribute during the Five Dynasties and the Qing period. Junshan yellow needle was a favorite of the eighteenth-century Emperor Qianlong, and the tea he enjoyed was probably close to the current version.

Junshan silver needle is the standard by which all other yellow teas are judged. It consists entirely of new sprouts picked in spring, guaranteeing a fine delicate flavor. Processing is similar to premium green tea except for two relatively short periods of oxidation. The leaves are stirred by hand in a warm wok, then heated again in a charcoal-heated stove. After initial drying, the tea is packed into bags and set aside for two days to oxidize slightly. Then the leaves undergo another heating in the oven and are once again packed into bags and allowed to oxidize for about twenty hours more. Finally, the leaves are heated one more time to stop oxidation and dry them out completely.

Junshan Silver Needle

Because this tea consists entirely of sprouts, it has a distinctive appearance. The dried leaves are straight, gray green, and come to a point at the tip, so they are said to resemble silver needles. The best leaves are uniform, plump, straight, and covered with down. The edges curl tightly inward toward the center, giving the leaf a slight bulge in the middle. Thin, twisted, and dark leaves indicate an inferior grade. Because Mount Junshan has little arable land, not much tea can be produced there, so top grade Junshan silver needle is always expensive.

Brewing these beautiful leaves in a glass pot allows drinkers to observe a strange phenomenon. When hot water is added, many leaves stand on end vertically at the bottom. Then they perform a little dance as they rise and sink repeatedly. (A popular saying has it that they "rise three times and sink three times.") The liquid ranges from light to dark yellow, depending upon strength. Overall, the fresh flavor of Junshan silver needle is close to green tea. The taste is extremely smooth and sweet, and has intriguing tones of seaweed and vanilla. This tea is famous for its fine sweet throat. The cold aroma lingering in the cup is also extremely sweet, reminiscent of honey, and intensifies considerably after a minute or two.

Meng Peak Yellow Sprout (*Mengding huangya*) 蒙頂黃芽

This is one of the world's oldest teas, dating back perhaps 1,800 years. Meng Peak was originally a green tea, and discerning literati singled it out for praise as early as the eleventh century. Sometime in the last few centuries, farmers began to oxidize the leaves slightly during processing, turning it into a yellow tea. The modern Meng Peak yellow sprout, sometimes called "sweet dew" (*ganlu*) or "stone flower" (*shihua*), is grown on a foggy five-peaked group of mountains known as Mengshan that stretches across Mingshan and Ya'an Counties in Sichuan. These mountains are part of the Qionglai range, whose unusual rainy climate is influenced by the enormously high peaks of neighboring Tibet. The area is dotted with old Buddhist temples, making it highly picturesque, although it now abuts the western suburbs of the enormous metropolis of Chengdu.

From the Tang through Qing dynasties, more than a thousand years in all, Meng Peak tea was often designated an item of imperial tribute, a testament to its enduring fame and quality. The ancient tradition of making tribute tea for China's rulers still endures. Each spring local officials dress in period costumes and personally harvest a small amount of tea. After conducting solemn rituals, Buddhist monks process the leaves in woks heated over charcoal. The final product is parceled out as gifts to China's leaders in Beijing.

The top grade of Meng Peak tea is produced entirely from sprouts. For second quality tea, one sprout and one leaf are harvested from each twig. During processing, the leaves are alternately heated in a wok and crinkled three times in succession. Next they are baked in an oven, allowed to oxidize slightly, then baked and oxidized again. This unique processing method gives the tea its unusual flavor. The finished leaves range in color from yellow to dark green and curl inward along their length. Because the leaves are so young, many are covered with fine down, although the light oxidation gives them a slight yellow tinge. The yellow liquid is fairly weak but pleasantly sweet and emits a beautiful fragrance somewhat like passion fruit. It has relatively little throat, however. According to legend, Meng Peak tea has remarkable curative powers and is sometimes consumed as medicine.

Huoshan Yellow Sprout (Huoshan *huangya*) 霍山黃芽

Huoshan is a mountain in Anhui Province that has lent its name to the surrounding County. The Tang dynasty tea master Lu Yu mentioned the area, and Huoshan tea has been prominent for more than a thousand years. The Qing emperors designated Huoshan tea an article of imperial tribute, but at some point production ceased for unknown reasons. In 1971, farmers in the area once again started growing yellow tea, and the revived Huoshan yellow sprout quickly reclaimed its reputation as one of China's outstanding brews. The best Huoshan yellow sprout comes from four spots on Huoshan called Jinjiwu, Jinshantou, Jinzhuping, and Wumijian. All are located at a fairly high altitude about 2,000 feet above sea level.

Tea is picked in the morning and processed in the afternoon. The leaves grown on Huoshan are extremely tender due to the cold mountain climate. Farmers take a sprout and one to three leaves from each twig. These are heated in a wok, baked, then allowed to oxidize for one or two days. Then they are baked again and given a second oxidation for another day or two, after which the tea is baked a final time until completely dry. The dried leaves are pale yellow green, slightly twisted, curl inward along the length of the leaf, and are covered with fine down. The highest grade consists of a sprout and leaf attached together in a *fleur-de-lis* shape called a sparrow tongue. Unlike other yellow teas, Huoshan yellow sprout should be brewed with relatively hot water at 90°–100° C (195°–215° F). The resulting yellow green liquid is sweet, very smooth, and topped off with a slight chestnut flavor.

Wanxi Yellow Big Tea (Wanxi *huang dacha*) 皖西黃大茶

This tea is produced in Huoshan, Liuan, Jinzhai, and Yuexi Counties of Anhui Province. This area was home to several famous green and yellow teas during the Ming dynasty. The finest of these, made from tender young sprouts, was an imperial tribute tea. Several kinds of tea are still grown there, including green, yellow, red, aged, and jasmine-scented varieties. Tea from the general area is often marketed as Liuan tea, even if it does not come specifically from Liuan County. Wanxi yellow big tea is grown near the Huoshan yellow sprout region. Since it is made from mature leaves, this is basically a lower grade version of that famous tea, and the taste is less refined.

If only a sprout and one or two leaves are harvested, farmers market it as "small tea" (*xiaocha*). The term "big tea" (*dacha*) is used when four or five leaves are taken along with each sprout. The leaves are picked in spring and summer. Not only are several leaves taken from each twig, but each leaf is also relatively large and thick. To process these unusual leaves, first they are heated repeatedly in a wok then baked in an oven for a few minutes, after which they are set out to oxidize for five to seven days. Finally, the leaves are baked again to stop oxidation and complete drying.

When dry, the plump mature leaves taper off into a curved golden stem that is said to resemble a fishhook. Wanxi yellow big tea comes in a number of grades, and these vary considerably in taste and quality. Because it is made from old leaves and the oxidation period is unusually long, the flavor is extremely strong for yellow tea. This tea is less common than before, as the taste is somewhat rough. However, some appreciate the strong flavor. The deep yellow liquid exudes a plantain aroma.

Beigang Hairy Points (Beigang *maojian*) 北港毛尖

Tea from the Beigang area on Lake Zi in Hunan was declared an imperial tribute article during the Tang dynasty, and connoisseurs praised it through the remainder of imperial history. Today this tea is mostly consumed in the cities of Yueyang, Changsha, and Wuhan. One sprout and two or three leaves are harvested from each twig. The tea is heated in a wok, crinkled, oxidized very briefly for 30–40 minutes, and tossed again over the fire. A final roasting in an oven dries it out completely. The leaves are golden yellow, plump, and come to a sharp point at the end. The liquid is orange yellow and has a clear fresh fragrance.

Luyuan Hairy Points (Luyuan *maojian*) 鹿苑毛尖

This tea comes from the area around the Luyuan Temple in Yuanan County, Hubei. The Tang connoisseur Lu Yu mentioned green tea from the area, and at some point farmers there started making yellow tea. Luyuan hairy sprouts was a tribute tea during the Qing dynasty and a particular favorite of the eighteenth-century Emperor Qianlong.

Farmers pick one sprout together with one or two leaves from each twig. Processing differs from most other yellow teas. Drying is done entirely in a wok, and the leaves are never baked. They are heated over a fire twice, allowed to oxidize for 5–6 hours, then stirred again over a flame until completely dry. Hairy points are named after the fine down covering the sharply tapered leaves. The leaves are noted for their golden hue, which is said to resemble the color of fish spawn. The yellow liquid is pleasantly sweet.

Wenzhou Yellow Soup (Wenzhou *huangtang*) 溫州黃湯

This tea is produced across a fairly large swath of southern Zhejiang Province, mostly in Taishun, Pingyang, Ruian, and Yongjia Counties. These places are not too far from the famous city of Wenzhou, traditionally the main market for this tea, and hence the name. The most sought after Wenzhou yellow soup comes from Dongxi in Taishun and Beigang in Pingyang. This tea was grown during the Qing dynasty, but production ceased for a time until it was revived in 1979.

A sprout and one or two leaves are picked from each twig. They are heated over an extremely hot fire and then crinkled. Next, the leaves are oxidized for two or three days, baked in an oven, then oxidized again for 3–4 hours. Drying is completed over a very low heat. The yellow-green leaves are quite thin and include a high proportion of young sprouts. This tea is said to be yellow in three different ways: yellow leaf, yellow stem, and yellow liquid. This tea boasts a clear, sharp aroma and fresh flavor.

Guangdong Big Leaf *qing* (Guangdong *daye qing*) 廣東大葉青

The term *qing* refers to an untranslatable color that can mean either green, blue, or blue green. Here it refers to the color of tea leaves from a particular hybrid. Guangdong big leaf is produced in Shaoguan, Qiqing, and Zhanjiang Counties in the subtropical region of southern Guangdong Province. The tea is picked in spring, summer, and autumn. During each flush, a sprout and two or three leaves are taken from each twig. The leaves are spread out on bamboo trays and dried indoors in a hot room, then heated in an extremely hot wok. After being rolled to crinkle them, the leaves are allowed to oxidize for a few hours and then heated twice more to complete drying. Guangdong big leaf *qing* is divided into five grades. The best leaves are plump and tightly curled. The liquid is dark yellow with a sweet flavor and clean fragrance.

Seahorse Palace Tea (Haimagong *cha*) 海馬宮茶

This tea is made in Dafang County, Guizhou at a place with the picturesque name Haimagong (Seahorse Palace). This area is cool enough for tea trees due to the high altitude, yet shielded from extreme cold by foggy mountains on three sides. For the premium variety of seahorse palace tea, just one leaf is harvested together with each sprout. Lesser grades use older leaves. The leaves are heated in a wok, rolled to crinkle them, oxidized for 24 hours, then heated and crinkled twice more. Finally, the leaves are baked in an oven at very low heat for more than 10 hours. The leaves are tightly curled, covered with down, and exude a rich aroma. Unlike most yellow teas, the color of the liquid is not yellow. Instead it exhibits a shade of green said to resemble the color of bamboo. The aftertaste is pleasantly sweet.

Weishan White Hairy Points (Weishan *baimaojian*) 溈山白毛尖

Weishan is an oddly shaped mountain in Ningxiang County, Hunan. A deep ravine runs along the top of the mountain for six miles, and this weird geological formation shelters a cold damp microclimate ideal for tea. Legend has it that Weishan tea was produced as early as the Tang dynasty. Its history during subsequent centuries was never recorded, but it was still around during the Qing dynasty.

The production method is somewhat unusual. A sprout and one or two leaves are picked from each twig. These are heated over a fire then oxidized for 6–8 hours. After being crinkled, they are baked to stop oxidation. The tea gets its unique flavor

from the last processing step. The leaves are sprayed with a mixture of water and tea oil, then set in a room heated by a smoldering fire to smoke for 16–20 hours. The finished leaves are green, covered with fine down, slightly curled, and somewhat oily. The yellow liquid is scented with a strong smoky flavor. Weishan tea has traditionally been sold to ethnic minorities in Gansu and Xinjiang who appreciate the odd smoky taste.

Chapter 8

Oolong Tea

The name oolong (*wulong*) refers to the large and varied family of semi-oxidized teas. Because oolongs fill the gap between green and red tea, many combine good qualities from both ends of the oxidation spectrum. Like good red tea, oolong can be extremely rich and smooth, but like green tea it preserves more of the plant's natural vegetable flavor. Because oolong covers the vast middle ground between green and red, it is by far the most diverse kind of tea. Some Taiwanese oolongs are lighter and more delicate than many green teas, while the strongest Fujian oolongs are heavier than the average red. The wide-ranging world of oolongs is fascinating to explore, and anyone can find a personal favorite.

Despite the current popularity of oolong, its origins are obscure. This style of tea is most closely identified with Fujian, where it was probably invented. Fujian teas were extremely popular with the elite during the Northern Song dynasty nine centuries ago, and a few iconoclastic scholars believe that those legendary classic teas were semi-oxidized oolongs. Nevertheless, the conventional view holds that Song teas were green and oxidation is a fairly recent innovation that became common in Fujian in the mid-nineteenth century.

Not only are the origins of semi-oxidized tea unclear but even the name oolong is quite mysterious. The name used in the West is an alternate spelling of the Chinese term *wulong*, which literally means "black dragon." One theory holds that this tea got its name because the leaves look like little black dragons, even though it is not at all clear how a tea leaf resembles a dragon. Another interpretation has it that "black dragon" was the nickname of a swarthy muscular tea farmer who helped popularize oxidized tea. To add to the confusion, because tea is usually categorized by color, Chinese sometimes refer to oolong as *qing* tea. *Qing* is an enigmatic color that can mean green, blue, or blue-green depending upon the context. Because English lacks this slippery chromatic concept, the more familiar term oolong is used here. Whatever we call it, good oolong is truly outstanding, and many Chinese connoisseurs consider premier oolongs the world's finest teas.

Although oolongs are produced here and there across China, most come from Fujian and from Taiwan. Tea from each place has an extremely different style. Fujian oolongs tend to be heavily oxidized until the leaves are dark green or brown, while Taiwan oolongs are only lightly oxidized so the leaves retain much of their original green color. In addition to these two major types, some good oolong is also produced in northern Guangdong, where the mountainous landscape resembles neighboring Fujian. Guangdong oolongs are extremely varied but tend to be somewhere in-between heavy Fujian oolongs and their much lighter Taiwanese cousins.

The first step in oolong appreciation is to grasp the fundamental differences between the Fujian and Taiwan styles of tea. The premium teas of both places are superb, but for different reasons. To draw a parallel with oil painting, Taiwanese oolongs seem like something that might have been created by Monet, while Fujian's oolongs are more like the work of a Rembrandt. Like Monet's paintings, Taiwanese oolongs are gorgeous crowd pleasers that are easy to understand and appreciate. They carry pretty fragrances like violet and lemon, retain quite a bit of the natural vegetable flavor, and are often sugarcane sweet. In contrast, Fujianese oolongs are much darker and heavier. A rich caramel sweetness is often overlaid with strong challenging flavors like cinnamon and camphor. Taiwanese teas are light and cheery while Fujianese oolongs tend to be moody and perhaps more profound. Generally speaking, Taiwan's oolongs are good for hot summer days, while their cousins from Fujian seem most satisfying in winter.

Oolongs of every stripe always taste best when brewed in a small pot. An Yixing teapot is ideal for this tea, as it brings out maximum flavor and fragrance. The water for Fujian oolongs should be just below boiling, although a temperature this high might bring out unpleasant acrid tones in the much lighter oolongs from Taiwan, which do much better with slightly cooler water at 80°–85° C (175°–185° F).

Fujian

As befits the homeland of semi-oxidized tea, Fujian produces a rich profusion of oolongs. Due to differences in climate, topography, and the use of different hybrids, teas from the northern and southern parts of the province are quite distinct. Almost all Fujian oolongs are heavily oxidized until they turn very dark green, brown, or even black. The leaves are usually crinkled and slightly curled and produce a strong, dense, oily liquid that is highly fragrant and flavorful with superb throat and impressive complexity. If brewed in a small pot, a top tea can be infused up to seven times.

Fujian became famous for its tea quite early, and most of China's emperors received tribute tea from the region. Northern Fujian was already producing notable teas in the ninth century, with the most renowned coming from the area around Mount Wuyi. During the Song dynasty, Wuyi was home to a famous tea plantation called the Northern Garden which produced tea for Emperor Song Huizong, the greatest imperial tea connoisseur. A local tea bureau continued to produce official tea during the Yuan dynasty.

Fujian oolong was exported to the West from the early seventeenth century onward. In Europe it was called *bohea*, which is the name of Mount Wuyi as pronounced in the Hokkien dialect spoken in Fujian. Before fully oxidized Indian-style red tea became predominant in the late nineteenth century, Fujian oolongs were extremely popular among European and North American drinkers. When we read about eighteenth-century Englishmen drinking afternoon tea, they were likely savoring Fujian oolong.

Wuyi Cliff Tea (Wuyi *yancha*) 武夷岩茶

Mount Wuyi on the northernmost edge of Fujian is surely the most amazing tea appellation in China. This impressive mountain has a circumference of forty miles and is said to consist of thirty-six peaks and ninety-nine cliffs. Up and down the crags, each spot shelters a unique microclimate that nurtures a slightly different variety of oolong. Besides variations in geography, many other factors come into play, including differences in the type of hybrid, harvest times, the minerals in each patch of soil, and methods for growing and processing. By tweaking numerous variables, the farmers of Mount Wuyi produce a dizzying array of teas with thousands of subtle gradations. One could easily devote a lifetime to exploring the universe of flavors and aromas that come from just this one mountain.

Cliff tea (*yancha*) is the generic name for Wuyi oolongs. This term comes from the fact that Wuyi farmers plant their tea within twisting couloirs and recesses sheltered by the mountain's cliffs and jagged boulders. Cliff tea is divided into three main types depending upon the tea field's geography: true cliff, half-cliff, and sand-bar. True cliff tea is produced among the cliffs of Mount Wuyi and usually has the richest flavor and best rhythm. Half-cliff tea is grown near the cliffs, but not among them, and is lower in quality. Sandbar tea is grown near mountain streams and is the humblest form of Wuyi cliff tea. In addition to this general geographical classification, cliff tea is also sometimes sold in four grades that are called (in descending order of quality) extraordinary, unique bush extraordinary, famous bush extraordinary, and famous. Cliff tea is also described according to the general style of processing or hybrid used, such as white cockscomb or iron arhat. And as if this were not already complicated, many cliff teas are also known by the names of flowers and plants that grow near the field (or used to grow nearby, or should have grown nearby) or by other fanciful terms. One author estimates that about 830 of these so-called "flower names" are used to classify different varieties of Wuyi cliff tea.

When we put these different classification systems together, the resulting nomenclature is incredibly specific but dauntingly complex. Extraordinary true cliff is different from unique bush extraordinary true cliff, while extraordinary true cliff white snow pear is not the same as extraordinary true cliff spring willow. No one knows for sure how many kinds of cliff tea are on the market, and the more teashops you visit, the more types you will discover. During the 1950s, government officials tried to simplify matters by dividing Wuyi tea into just three general grades: prime, fine, and rough. With the revival of China's tea culture, however, the bewildering but highly specific system of traditional names has come back into use.

Wuyi tea is the archetypal northern Fujian oolong. During the harvest, either three or four leaves are usually picked from each stem. First, the leaves are placed in large flat baskets to dry them in the sun for an hour or two, then they are moved inside, placed in deep baskets, and allowed to oxidize for 8–12 hours. The leaves are stirred in a hot wok twice, crinkled after each heating, and finished off by baking twice in a hot oven.

The resulting dry leaves look twisted and dark green. As they age, the leaves steadily darken to become brown then black. When rehydrated they often exhibit small white bumps that connoisseurs compare to frog skin or oyster shell. High grade Wuyi cliff tea is truly extraordinary in quality. The scent and flavor of the yellow liquid are extremely rich, and the tea has excellent throat. A prominent natural caramel sweetness is overlaid with numerous flavors that vary enormously between fields, depending upon the particular microclimate and minerals absorbed from the rocky soil. Although these varied tastes and scents are difficult to summarize, a lovely orchid fragrance is often present. Cliff tea is famous for its rhythm, often referred to as "cliff rhythm," and each infusion brings new tastes to the forefront.

Old cliff tea is also available, and ageing usually considerably intensifies the flavor. In recent years some producers have revived the Fujian tea disks that were the rage a thousand years ago. These compressed disks, similar to Yunnan *puer*, make ageing more convenient. Loose-leaf and compressed tea are both aged. Be forewarned that some aged Fujian tea will shock the uninitiated. I have tasted a fine ten year old cliff tea that had a gorgeously rich fragrance, but the flavor had become almost numbingly strong. Because of its intimidating potency, this sort of aged cliff tea is definitely an acquired taste. The novice might be terrified by its hair-curling power, but connoisseurs consider strong old cliff tea well suited for cold winter days. However, other ageing methods can produce old tea that is rich but mellow and easily approachable.

Big Red Robe (Wuyi *da hongpao*) 武夷大紅袍.

The most famous Wuyi tea is surrounded by mystery. If you look credulous, a teashop owner might tell you that big red robe is grown by Buddhist monks on inaccessible cliffs and picked by their trained monkeys. Others will tell you that it comes from enormously tall trees and has magical healing properties. In truth, no one is quite sure about the origins of this tea, and there are three explanations for its colorful name. One version holds that it was originally picked by trained monkeys that wore red vests so that the farmers could distinguish them from their wild cousins. According to another story, after this miraculous tea cured a scholar of his illness, he traveled to Mount Wuyi, took off his red silk robe, and laid it before the tea trees as a gift to express his gratitude. A more prosaic explanation attributes the name to the unusual yellow purple color of the leaves.

Big Red Robe

Even after discounting all the fantastic tales surrounding big red robe, it is still a remarkable tea produced under unusual conditions. The rarest and most expensive tea in the world, it is virtually impossible to obtain. Authentic big red robe comes from an extremely high spot on Mount Wuyi called Nine Dragon Nest, which lies above precipitous Celestial Heart Cliff. Water from an underground spring constantly dribbles out of the rocks and irrigates a dense carpet of lichens and moss on top of the cliff. As the moss dies, it steadily decays into a rich organic fertilizer that nourishes a few tea trees growing among the crags. Properly speaking, only tea from a few ancient trees there, said to be more than 350 years old, can be called big red robe. Some people say that big red robe comes from just three trees, others say four, while the most generous allow the leaves from six trees to be counted as the genuine article. Because this tea is so rare and expensive, the trees are kept under constant guard and visitors cannot even touch them. Of course, harvesting and processing are absolutely meticulous, and the resulting product is the very highest grade of Wuyi cliff tea. The leaves of big red robe can supposedly be infused nine times before losing their floral scent. Many consider it the finest tea in the world.

Unfortunately, due to its almost legendary reputation, counterfeit big red robe far outnumbers the real thing. Only a few pounds of big red robe are produced annually, and this usually ends up in the hands of powerful people with special connections. In fact, some say that the entire harvest of big red robe is monopolized by high government officials, and all of the tea publicly marketed under this name is fake. I have no way of knowing whether this is true or not, but buyers should be extremely cautious. It is said that the scent of authentic big red robe is reminiscent of *osmanthus* blossoms, and this might be a way of checking for authenticity. Real or not, tea marketed as big red robe is always very expensive. If you buy it from a reputable dealer, at least you will probably end up with some premium Wuyi tea, but you have no way of knowing whether or not it was actually grown in Nine Dragon Nest. In any case, few people will be willing to pay for the real thing. In 2004, a small amount of genuine big red robe was sold at auction in Hong Kong to commemorate the anniversary of a local tea organization. The tea was a gift from the Wuyi government, so it was unquestionably authentic. Twenty grams (0.71 ounce) sold for 166,000 HK dollars (about USD 21,283).

Iron Arhat (Wuyi *tie luohan*) 武夷鐵羅漢

This famous variety of fine cliff tea has been around for about 150 years. Originally iron arhat referred to tea made from a special big leaf tree grown in a place called Ghost Hole, a small valley between steep cliffs that is irrigated by a small stream. During the nineteenth century, a teashop started offering iron arhat as its premium Wuyi cliff tea and claimed that the tea had miraculous curative powers. It became so popular that farmers from other parts of Mount Wuyi began calling their tea iron arhat too. Now this name refers to any Wuyi tea made from the type of hybrid originally grown in Ghost Hole. This tea carries notes of seaweed and spinach.

White Cockscomb (Wuyi *bai jiguan*) 武夷白雞冠

This tea has been around since the Ming dynasty. On the tree, the leaves of this hybrid have a lighter color than most of the tea grown on Mount Wuyi. When wet, the green leaves are edged with a reddish purple rim. According to legend, the son of an official traveling through the Wuyi area took sick and was cured by a monk who used this tea as medicine. The monk called his medicinal tea white cockscomb. Later the official sent some of this amazing tea to the emperor as a gift, and the grateful sovereign rewarded the monk with a generous stipend. Some say that the white cockscomb hybrid originated in Ghost Hole alongside iron arhat, while others claim that it was first grown near Wuyi Temple. Besides these two areas, the white cockscomb hybrid is now grown elsewhere on Mount Wuyi as well.

White cockscomb is the most lightly oxidized cliff tea, giving it a delicate flavor unique among Fujian teas. The greenish liquid tastes somewhat like a Taiwanese high mountain oolong. This tea is noted for its gorgeous scent, which has an impressively strong orchid aroma in addition to other floral and fruit tones. The flavor is light, sweet, slightly sour, and acrid, with notes of seaweed and chestnut. This unusual combination of flavors and scents emerge one after another, giving it superb rhythm.

Golden Water Turtle (Wuyi *shui jingui*) 武夷水金龜

This is another premium cliff tea. According to legend, monks originally planted golden water turtle trees on a cliff beneath Dugezhai Peak. The branches of two of these trees intertwined, forming a shape that resembled a turtle. This hybrid gained notice for its outstanding taste, which is easy for beginners to appreciate because of the intense floral scents and sweet citrus character. Landslides during the 1920s caused the cliffs in this tea's original range to collapse, so golden water turtle is now grown at another spot on Mount Wuyi called Orchid Valley Cliff. The price is reasonable for good Wuyi cliff tea, which is never cheap, and considering the superb flavor this tea is an excellent value.

Wuyi Cinnamon (Wuyi *rougui*) 武夷肉桂

This tea is also sometimes called vermilion cinnamon or jade cinnamon. Whatever name is used, this is a premium cliff tea harvested from a hybrid originally grown near Wisdom Garden Cliff or Mazhen Peak. Now the same variety of tea tree is raised in many places across Mount Wuyi. These trees are unusually large and are allowed to grow more than 6 feet tall. As the name implies, it has a noticeable cinnamon taste and overall the flavor is stronger than most cliff teas. In addition, Wuyi cinnamon carries strong floral and fruit scents as well as a natural sweetness that all balance out the somewhat harsh cinnamon flavor. This tea has excellent rhythm, throat, and endurance. The hearty cinnamon taste makes it an excellent choice for cold winter days. Some people say that it can be used as a substitute for real cinnamon in concoctions of Chinese herbal medicine.

Octagonal Pavilion Dragon Whiskers (*bajiaoting longxu*) 八角亭龍須

The leaves of this tea are usually tied into small bundles said to resemble the whiskers on a dragon's chin. Dragon whiskers were being grown on Mount Wuyi in the early eighteenth century. Today this tea is still grown in the Wuyi area as well as in surrounding places in Chang'an and Jianou Counties. The tea grown at a place called Octagonal Pavilion on Mount Wuyi is said to produce the best dragon whiskers tea. Leaves are harvested in spring and early summer, and one sprout together with three or four leaves are taken from each stem. Processing is similar to regular cliff tea. The finished leaves are relatively straight and range in color from dark green to black. As a final flourish, the leaves are tied up with string into tiny bundles less than half an ounce each. Dragon whiskers produce a rich yellow brew redolent with floral aromas.

North Fujian Water Immortal (*Minbei shuixian*) 閩北水仙

Aside from the many types of cliff tea, another highly regarded oolong from northern Fujian is water immortal tea, which has been grown since the nineteenth century. This name refers to any tea descended from a hybrid discovered in Jianyang County, Fujian. According to legend, water immortal tea got its name because the original tree was discovered growing wild by a farmer while visiting a shrine to a local Daoist deity. "Water immortal" is a homonym for the phrase "sacrificing to an immortal" in the local Hokkien dialect, and this misunderstanding supposedly resulted in the present name. These trees grow to be extremely large and can reach a height of up to 16 feet. The flowers are also unusually big and the leaves are quite thick. Today water immortal is grown in the northern and southern regions of Fujian as well as northern Guangdong. Although all tea by this name comes from the same hybrid, water immortal from each of its three main regions differs considerably because of variations in climate and topography. Northern Fujian water immortal is produced in several places, including the famous Mount Wuyi.

Northern Fujian water immortal is harvested year round, but tea sellers usually distinguish four flushes: spring, summer, autumn, and "dew" tea (also called winter dew tea). A sprout and three or four leaves are harvested from each stem. The processing method is similar to cliff tea, although sometimes water immortal is not crinkled, so the dried leaves end up fairly flat. Some leaves are curled at only one end and taper out to a flat surface, a shape referred to as "dragonfly head and frog leg." Northern Fujian water immortal yields a fragrant rich yellow liquid that often carries strong floral scents such as orchid. The flavor is very rich and has good throat. This tea ages well, and if stored properly the sweetness intensifies after a few years.

Anxi Iron Bodhisattva (Anxi *tie Guanyin*) 安溪鐵觀音

The most famous teas of southern Fujian are produced in Anxi County, a mountainous area above the port city of Quanzhou. Green tea has been grown there since the Tang dynasty, and in the past century Anxi has become major source of oolong. Prior to the rise of red tea, it was also very popular abroad. At the height of its international popularity during the nineteenth century, British merchants bought 4,500 tons of Anxi oolong every year.

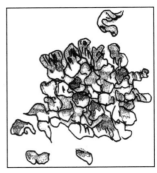

Anxi Iron Bodhisattva

This region is home to more than fifty tea hybrids, each producing a somewhat different beverage. The most famous Anxi tea is iron bodhisattva, which dates back to the early Qing dynasty. This tea owes its characteristic flavor, heavy yet sweet, to a special hybrid native to the region. The origins of this tea are disputed. According to legend, once there was a pious farmer who often sacrificed to the Bodhisattva Guanyin (also known as Avalokiteshvara). One day while he was out chopping wood, the farmer came across a strange new kind of tea tree growing in the forest. This wild tree had unusually large flowers and thick leaves said to be as heavy as iron, and it yielded excellent tea. The farmer considered this marvelous tea a reward for his religious devotion so he called it iron bodhisattva. Other stories maintain that the tea got its name because it was discovered at a place called Guanyin Cliff or near an iron statue of Guanyin.

Iron bodhisattva is harvested in four flushes: spring, summer, high summer, and autumn. As usual, the spring flush is best. Processing is similar to Wuyi cliff tea. The leaves are dark green, curled, heavy, and turn dark brown then black with age. Unlike cliff tea, iron bodhisattva is often rolled into balls, giving it a more intense flavor in the first infusion. Premium leaves tend to have spots of green or red, or else light streaks called "white frost." The rich amber liquid is very robust. Iron bodhisattva is one of the most intensely fragrant teas, with notes of camphor balanced out by a strong orchid scent. The flavor has tones of caramel and a milky richness. Good iron bodhisattva has excellent endurance and can be infused seven times in a small pot. It is famous for a sweet throat reminiscent of honey.

Since the late nineteenth century, farmers in Muzha, Taipei County, Taiwan have grown a small amount of tea that they call iron bodhisattva, although this term has a somewhat different meaning in Taiwan. Although most Fujian iron bodhisattva is grown around Anxi and is closely identified with it, the name as used in Fujian basically refers, in fact, to tea that comes from a specific hybrid. In Taiwan, however, any tea that tastes somewhat like the Anxi original is called iron bodhisattva. The Taiwanese version tends to be baked longer during processing, giving it a slightly stronger flavor than its Anxi namesake.

Yellow Gold *osmanthus* (*huangjin gui*) 黃金桂

This tea comes from another distinctive hybrid tree from Anxi County in southern Fujian. Legend has it that in the mid-nineteenth century a local tea farmer discovered an odd-looking wild tea tree covered with unusually pretty blossoms and delicate leaves. He brought it home and kept it as a decorative potted plant, where it attracted notice from visitors who admired its beauty. When he made tea from the leaves, the farmer was astonished to discover that they produced an unusually fragrant brew with an intense floral scent. People in the region considered this hybrid a priceless treasure, and the original tree was kept alive until 1967. Nowadays, many trees propagated from the original plant are still grown around Anxi.

The harvest time is especially important for yellow gold *osmanthus*. If picked too early the tea will be acrid, but if too late it will produce an insipid brew. The premium grade is usually harvested during a short period in mid-April when two or three leaves are taken from each stem. Lower grades are made from tea harvested during four or five flushes at other times of year. Besides the first-rate spring flush, the autumn tea is also well regarded. The curled dried leaves are yellow-green and edged with red. Because the level of oxidation is lower than other Fujian teas, yellow gold *osmanthus* is relatively light. The sweet golden liquid has a strong floral scent like *osmanthus* blossoms and a rich tangerine flavor.

Anxi colored tea (Anxi sezhong) 安溪色種

The name "colored" tea is very vague and basically refers to all of the lesser oolongs from the Anxi area of southern Fujian. Harvesting and processing are similar to iron bodhisattva, but the tea comes from different hybrids so each has a distinctive appearance and taste. There are five main types of colored tea and several dozen lesser varieties.

Native mountain (*benshan*) 本山 is close to iron bodhisattva but somewhat lighter. The leaves of hairy crab (*maoxie*) 毛蟹 are covered with fine white down and have a natural jasmine flavor. Strange orchid (*qilan*) 奇蘭 has a pure sweet flavor. Plum dew (*meizhan*) 梅占 is known for its intense aroma. There is also a variety called colored oolong tea (*sezhong wulong*) 色種烏龍. In this instance "oolong" is used as the proper name for this specific Anxi hybrid, which is distinguished by a delicate caramel scent.

Yongchun Buddha Hand (Yongchun *foshou*) 永春佛手
Aside from the teas of Anxi, another noteworthy oolong from southern Fujian comes from nearby Yongchun County. The leaves of this unusual local hybrid resemble those of a citrus tree called the Buddha hand citron. It is unclear where this hybrid originated, and some say it is native to a cliff in the remarkable Anxi area. In fact, there are two types of Buddha hand tea that come from closely related hybrids, called red sprout Buddha hand and green sprout Buddha hand after the color of their young leaves. A version of this tea was being produced by the early eighteenth century.

One sprout and two or three leaves are harvested from each stem, and the leaves are unusually large and heavy. There are four flushes: spring, summer, high summer, and autumn. Processing is similar to most other Fujian oolongs, except that the sitting time is reduced because the leaves oxidize so quickly. The dried leaves of Yongchun Buddha hand are plump, curled, and covered with green bumps. The flavor of the yellow orange liquid is strong and sweet. Sometimes Yongchun Buddha hand tea is put inside a hollowed out pomelo skin and allowed to age for several years until both peel and tea are black. As the pomelo peel dries and shrinks, it compresses the leaves inside into a dense solid mass. The resulting tea has a strong flavor and pleasant citrus fragrance, and is said to have gained powerful medicinal qualities.

Taiwan

Taiwanese farmers imported trees and growing techniques from Fujian during the nineteenth century and refined them to suit local conditions and tastes, creating their own version of oolong tea. The quality of Taiwan's tea is largely due to the island's unusual geography. Although the climate of lowland Taiwan is subtropical, the highest mountains in Asia east of Tibet bisect the island. The unusual combination of hot humid plains and very high mountains gives Taiwan an unusually diverse climate that geographers describe as "three-dimensional." Almost every environment can be found on Taiwan, from tropical beaches on the southern tip to snowy alpine peaks at the highest elevations. Within this rich ecological diversity, farmers have discovered many niches perfectly suited for tea.

Taiwanese farmers and processors are extremely innovative. While China was being torn apart by political chaos through most of the twentieth century, tea specialists on Taiwan could still devote their full attention to experimenting with new hybrids and techniques. Today Taiwanese tea-making combines meticulous labor-intensive farming with high-tech mechanical processing. Whereas mainland farmers usually heat tea leaves in huge woks and charcoal-fired ovens, almost all Taiwanese tea is machine processed. In addition, packaging and marketing are far ahead of mainland China. The resulting product is much more uniform than traditional Chinese tea, and very little is ruined owing to faulty handling, although this high-tech approach inevitably sacrifices some of the intriguing idiosyncrasies that distinguish a completely handmade product.

Although Taiwan exported huge amounts of oolong during the first half of the twentieth century, labor costs are now much higher than in other tea producing regions, so Taiwanese tea has been priced out of the global mass market. Fortunately, there is still an enthusiastic domestic market for high-quality local tea and Taiwan abounds with elegant teahouses and well appointed teashops. Sophisticated domestic consumers have demanded constant refinement of the island's oolongs.

Today there are several on-going trends in the Taiwanese tea world. Oxidation is a topic of endless controversy. Some drinkers complain that Taiwanese oolongs have become too light and are now uncomfortably close to green tea. The ideal degree of sweetness is another source of disagreement. Some Taiwanese oolongs carry so much natural sweetness that it is hard to believe that no sugar has been added. While some people enjoy these sugary teas, others complain that they offer too much of a good thing. Critics call for more bitterness to balance out these sweet oolongs, or else urge farmers to confine most of the sweetness to the throat.

New teas are also a major topic of controversy. In the past, Taiwanese farmers usually tried to imitate famous mainland teas, in some cases improving the originals. Now some tea experts insist that Taiwanese should break with tradition and exploit the island's unusual geography and climate to produce innovative teas unlike anything grown elsewhere. A few unique new teas have already hit the market, displaying impressive ingenuity. This is definitely a trend to watch.

The best Taiwanese oolongs are now extremely expensive, so counterfeiting has become a major problem. Large quantities of Taiwan-style oolong are being grown in China and Vietnam and pawned off on gullible consumers as Taiwanese tea. Anyone buying expensive Taiwanese tea should be cautious. Counterfeit tea is not necessarily bad, but, of course, consumers deserve to get what they are paying for. Buying only from reputable shops is the best way to avoid being saddled with fake tea.

Taiwanese oolongs are numerous, and the distinctions among them can be somewhat subtle. Unfortunately, the classification of semi-oxidized Taiwanese teas is inconsistent, with three different methods in use. Some teas are classified more or less according to style (such as *baozhong* or generic "high mountain" tea), others according to place (like Alishan and Shanlinxi), while another method uses the name of the tea hybrid (blue jade and golden lily). Sometimes the systems are combined to produce a longer and more specific name like Alishan *jinxuan* or Nangang *baozhong*. The only way to familiarize yourself with the various types of Taiwanese oolong is to be adventurous and start tasting different teas. Here I will introduce some of the major Taiwan oolongs, going generally from the lighter varieties to the stronger.

Baozhong (or *pouchong*) 包種

This delicate tea, oxidized only about 15%, is far lighter than any oolong from Fujian and, in fact, is very close to green tea. The name *baozhong* means "wrapped type" tea and refers to a former paper package. During the nineteenth century *baozhong* was exported in huge quantities prior to the vogue for dark Indian tea, and in the West it was often marketed under the alternate spellings *pouchong* or *pouching*. Today relatively little of this tea leaves Taiwan because of its the high price.

There are two kinds of *baozhong*, Wenshan and Nangang. Most *baozhong* belongs to the Wenshan type, the heavier of the two. It is grown on mountains around the town of Pinglin in Taipei County where settlers from Fujian first began growing tea in the eighteenth century. There are three flushes a year (spring, autumn, and winter). As usual, the spring tea is the best. Nangang *baozhong* is grown in a district of suburban Taipei by that name. It has been produced since about 1885, but today very little is grown.

The medium green leaves of *baozhong* oolong are usually naturally curled instead of rolled, and high quality leaves are covered with tiny grayish

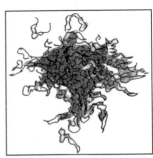

Wenshan Baozhong

white spots that connoisseurs have nicknamed frog skin. *Baozhong* is so delicate that it absolutely must be brewed in a cup or small pot. Steeping these leaves in a large Western-style teapot will produce an almost flavorless liquid. Most Taiwanese drink *baozhong* in a small Yixing pot, but I think that a covered cup also suits this light tea. The pale yellow brew has an ethereal taste topped off by elegant aromas such as orchid and lemon. *Baozhong* is less oily than other Taiwanese oolongs, giving it a sense of lightness and purity. Although *baozhong* is usually consumed hot, it also makes excellent iced tea.

New Hybrids

Taiwan's government has long subsidized research into new tea tree hybrids, and much of the tea produced on the island now comes from unique trees unlike anything traditionally grown in mainland China. Various new hybrids are widely grown across north and central Taiwan. Considering how expensive Taiwanese oolongs can be, tea from these new hybrids is usually quite reasonably priced considering the quality, so many Taiwanese consume it as their main daily beverage.

The word *cui* in the name blue jade (*cuiyu*) 翠玉 refers to the unique shimmering blue-green color of the kingfisher's feathers and is often used to describe exceptionally beautiful jade. Blue jade tea has a delicate flavor and an attractive floral fragrance. The taste of golden lily (*jinxuan*) 金萱 is unique among oolongs, with a rich milky flavor and fragrant tones of vanilla, narcissus, and citrus. All eternal spring (*siji chun*) 四季春 trees are descended from a single natural mutation discovered on one of Taiwan's tea farms. The rich aroma is sometimes compared to gardenia.

High Mountain Oolong (*gaoshan wulong*) 高山烏龍

The mountains of central Taiwan are home to the island's most celebrated teas, which have been collectively called high mountain oolong since the 1970s. The unique climate of central Taiwan is perfect for tea, and minerals in the rocky soil give these oolongs superb complexity and rhythm. In general, the higher the tea field, the more subtle the flavor. Inexperienced drinkers will probably prefer tea from lower elevations, as it is more assertive and easier to appreciate, but connoisseurs prize the ineffable "softness" of tea from the highest elevations. High mountain oolongs are some of the world's finest teas, so they are never cheap. Consumers pay a premium for teas from the highest elevations.

A sprout and two to four leaves are harvested from each twig, depending upon the quality of the tea to be produced. These are usually oxidized about 25%, giving a medium green color. The leaves are customarily rolled into balls to give them more initial intensity. Even so, unlike most balled teas, good high mountain oolong still displays superb rhythm and endurance and the leaves can be infused up to seven times. The liquid is very pale yellow and slightly oily. This tea maintains the plant's natural vegetable flavor overlaid with traces of sugarcane, milk, floral aromas such as orchid, and fruit fragrances such as pear.

Taiwan High Mountain Oolong

Lesser tea is sold as generic high mountain oolong; better quality leaves are usually identified by the name of the place they were grown. However, even if a specific place name is given, this is still no more than a general clue as to the quality and characteristics that can be expected. Like Mount Wuyi, each of the famous Taiwanese tea mountains has fields with different microclimates and elevations, and the chemical composition of the soil varies significantly from place to place, so each spot produces distinctive tea. Some dealers will even distinguish a particular location on a mountain because, for example, Pear Mountain tea from Fushoushan at an altitude of 7,200 feet and Hongxiang at 4,200 feet taste very different. Like the varied teas of Mount Wuyi in Fujian, you could happily spend a lifetime exploring the fascinating world of Taiwan's high mountain oolongs.

Winter Peak (*dongding*) Oolong 凍頂烏龍
This tea is grown around the town of Lugu among the mountains of Nantou County. The trees there are descended from saplings brought over from Mount Wuyi in 1885. The taste varies somewhat depending upon location, harvest time, processing method, and the farmer's individual ingenuity, but premium winter peak oolong is superb. The flavor is pure and light, with sugarcane sweetness well balanced by a pleasant hint of bitterness. This tea's sublime fragrance is often compared to the delicate scent of gardenia. Unfortunately, much of the prime tea growing land in Lugu was destroyed during the catastrophic 1999 earthquake.

Alishan Oolong 阿里山烏龍
This tea is produced on rocky cliffs in the area around the scenic mountain by that name, located in Chiayi County. Intrepid tea farmers are planting crops at ever higher

altitudes, so more of this excellent tea is coming on the market. Alishan tea is always in high demand, and the finest leaves are fabulously expensive. The leaves have a sugarcane aroma when dry, but when wet they release a powerful orchid scent.

There are also several minor regional high mountain oolongs that are usually quite expensive because of their rarity. Almost all of this tea is consumed in Taiwan because few people elsewhere are willing to pay such a high price.

- **Pear Mountain (Lishan) Oolong** 梨山烏龍 comes from another mountain in Nantou County famous for its pear orchards. Excellent oolong has been grown there since the 1970s. There are spring and winter flushes. Pear Mountain is very large and produces the highest altitude Taiwanese oolong.
- **Shanlinxi Oolong** 杉林溪烏龍 is grown on the precipitously steep slopes of another mountainous area of Nantou. The difficulty of growing tea under such perilous conditions justifies its high price. There are four flushes a year, and the spring flush is the best. The finest Shanlinxi tea is intensely sweet and highly aromatic, with tones of pomelo and cedar.
- **Dayuling Oolong** 大禹嶺烏龍 is produced in a small quantity among the mountains of the western part of Hualian County. Its sweet flavor is topped off with floral and tangerine scents.

Muzha Iron Bodhisattva (Muzha *tie Guanyin*) 木柵鐵觀音

This oolong has been produced in the Maokong Valley near the town of Muzha in Taipei County since the early twentieth century, when Taiwan was still a Japanese colony. It is supposedly an imitation of the original iron bodhisattva grown in Anxi in southern Fujian, but, in fact, different hybrids are used so the flavor is fairly distinct. Muzha iron bodhisattva is oxidized about 40% and baked longer than its Fujian namesake, yielding a medium orange brew. Despite its strength, the flavor is relatively gentle and sweet. It has admirable complexity together with excellent rhythm and throat. Unfortunately, less iron bodhisattva is being grown around Muzha nowadays, so it is becoming increasingly expensive.

Oriental Beauty (*dongfang meiren*) 東方美人

This tea is grown in the Wenshan District of Taipei County. In the early twentieth century, most of the harvest was exported to the West where it was marketed under the old-fashioned name Oriental beauty. In Taiwan, it is often called white down oolong (*baihao wulong*) after the large number of young white leaves. This is the strongest of the major Taiwanese oolongs and is about 70% oxidized. Even so, it still maintains a characteristic Taiwanese delicacy that distinguishes it from the heartier oolongs of Fujian. The flavor is somewhat like red tea but much lighter, and its wonderful sweet aroma made it popular in foreign markets back when Taiwan was still a major tea exporter. Some Europeans declared Oriental beauty the champagne of teas, and it is sometimes still called champagne oolong.

Those European drinkers may have been more reserved in their praise if they had heard the myths about this tea. Some people say that Oriental beauty's unique flavor comes from being nibbled by a species of beetle known as *fuluzi* ("floating deer"). Juices excreted by the beetle's jaws supposedly interact with enzymes in the leaf to give it a sweet flavor (or so the story goes). The leaves are small and slightly twisted, but not crinkled or rolled. The leaves come in five different colors: white, green, yellow, red, and black. High quality Oriental beauty includes many young white buds covered with down. This tea is a fairly heavy and produces a red liquid. The flavor is extremely similar to Sun Moon red tea, except that Oriental beauty also carries additional acrid notes that are not at all unpleasant. It has a very rich sweet flavor and excellent throat.

Pingdong Harbor Tea (Pingdong *gangkou cha*) 屏東港口茶
Although this inexpensive tea grown near the coast of Pingdong County in far south Taiwan is not very good, it still rates a passing mention because of its odd flavor. Whereas most Taiwanese oolongs are grown on high mountains, this tea comes from fields in a relatively low-lying area near the sea. The leaves absorb some of the flavor of the sea air as they grow, giving the liquid a startling salty taste.

Guangdong

Phoenix Tea (Fenghuang *cha*) 鳳凰茶
This is the only notable oolong from Guangdong, where it is produced in the northern part of the province near the border with Fujian. Phoenix tea tends to be much lighter than the Fujian oolongs but not nearly as light as most of the teas from Taiwan. Guangdong oolong is called phoenix tea after the Phoenix (Fenghuang) Mountains, part of a range with more than fifty peaks that pass through the Chaoan area and neighboring counties where it is grown. Tea has been produced there for more than 900 years. Phoenix tea has traditionally been consumed mostly in Guangdong and southern Fujian and is now quite popular in Hong Kong. The two major types are Phoenix and Lingtou, and the tea from each place is often marketed in three grades: unique bush, wavy, and water immortal. The name "unique bush"

refers to the genetic diversity of the tea plants grown in the Phoenix Mountains. Every plant there is said to be unique, and even two trees next to each other can produce very different tea.

The leaves of phoenix tea are long and twisted, and the shape supposedly resembles bird beaks. Others compare the shape of the leaves to rolled up slivers of eel skin. A small amount is compressed into bricks for ageing. The hybrids grown in the Phoenix Mountains are related to Fujian water immortal tea farther north but seem closer to a common wild ancestor. In fact, due to the numerous variations among tea trees in the area, it is difficult to characterize phoenix tea. Many dealers come up with fanciful names (such as yellow branch and honey orchid) to label a particular batch. Some types are extremely light and their leaves are almost white. Others are oxidized to a medium degree and the green leaves can show streaks of yellow or crimson. There are even feral tea trees, some of which are 400 years old, whose leaves produce very idiosyncratic brews. Because phoenix oolong is so unpredictable, it is always a good idea to taste a sample before you buy so you know what you are getting.

This tea is picked four times a year (spring, summer, autumn, and winter). The winter flush is sometimes called "snowflake" tea. During processing the leaves are spread out on broad shallow trays and placed in a warm dry place to let some of the moisture gradually evaporate. Then the trays are returned to a normal atmosphere to cool. Sometimes this process is repeated. The tea is then allowed to oxidize, stirred in a hot wok, crinkled, then slowly baked three times to finish drying. Whatever the variety, phoenix tea is extremely sweet and mellow, pleasantly balanced with a slight bitterness, somewhat acrid, and imbued with complex refreshing flavors like green apple, peach, and grape. Lingtou tea often carries a honeyed fragrance.

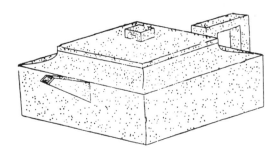

Chapter 9

Red Tea

The longer tea leaves oxidize after being harvested, the darker they become. When oxidation is carried through to the end, eventually all the enzymes in the leaf bond with oxygen and the process naturally stops. Westerners call fully oxidized leaves black tea after the color of the leaves, or English tea after its most famous fans. In contrast, Chinese describe fully oxidized tea by the color of the liquid instead of the leaves, hence the name red tea. Although Indian and Sri Lankan (Ceylon) reds are now most famous, this processing method was invented in Fujian, and China still produces vast amounts of red tea. Most Chinese reds are only middling quality, destined to end up in mass market blends, but farmers also grow small quantities of superb premium reds comparable to the best teas from South Asia.

Even though red tea is not especially popular with Chinese consumers, the export market is enormous and so oxidized teas are grown in an immense area that stretches across twelve provinces. By Chinese standards, red tea is a fairly new invention. Some claim that small amounts were being made in the early Ming dynasty. Whenever it began, full oxidation did not become common until the nineteenth century when foreign demand spurred production. Red tea is more stable than other varieties and unlikely to go bad on long ocean voyages, which probably explains why it became so popular in distant foreign markets.

Complete oxidation covers up most of the plant's natural flavor, so red tea is often made from inferior old leaves. For most reds, a sprout and two to five leaves are taken from each twig. Premium reds (such as high grade Keemun) are usually picked while young and have very small leaves. Chinese reds are divided into three main types: *gongfu*, *xiaozhong* (smoked), and red brick tea. Most reds, including the finest varieties, are categorized as *gongfu*. There is only one notable *xiaozhong* tea—the strange smoky *lapsang souchong*. Compressed red brick teas, not highly regarded, only date back to 1958. *Gongfu* teas are subdivided into big leaf and small leaf. Most big leaf *gongfu* reds come from Yunnan and are taken from feral trees like those that yield black *puer* tea. Small leaf *gongfu*, sometimes called black leaf *gongfu*, refers to reds harvested from standard cultivated varieties. *Gongfu* teas are further classified by region, usually vaguely labeled by province, and tea from each area is typically divided into seven grades of quality.

Red tea is processed like oolong but with a much longer oxidation period. Also, since red tea is a mass produced export commodity, it is often machine processed in large factories, unlike most Chinese teas, which are prepared in small batches by hand. To make *gongfu* tea, first the leaves are withered, usually by a device that blows them with hot air, until about 40% of the moisture is removed. Then they are crushed to expose the inner enzymes to air and left in a warm and humid place until fully oxidized. Finally, the leaves are heated in an oven to stop oxidation and dry them out completely.

Allowing the leaves to oxidize fully gives red tea its characteristic dark color and rich mellow flavor. Completing the full cycle of oxidation also gives reds a somewhat different chemical composition from other teas. Red tea is full of flavonoids, a chemical also found in red wine and cocoa, which accounts for its rich taste. Scientific research suggests that some flavonoids are anti-oxidants, anti-inflammatories, and might even help prevent cancer.

Despite relatively uniform processing, Chinese reds vary considerably in quality and characteristics. All are full-bodied and often carry a caramel sweetness together with other flavors and scents. Some reds are intentionally complex and even slightly bitter in the style of sophisticated Assam teas, while others are extremely smooth and recall the delicate reds of Darjeeling.

Foreign tastes and technology have had a major impact on China's red teas. Sometimes leaves processed for export are mechanically chopped into a coarse uniform powder in imitation of Indian teas. However, domestically consumed reds are almost always left as whole leaves so that the flavors are released more gradually, giving the tea more rhythm. Whereas Westerners routinely add milk and sugar to red tea, Chinese usually drink it straight. Red tea tastes best in a small pot but is strong enough for a larger brewing vessel. The water should be on the hot side, 90°–100° C (195°–215° F).

Keemun (Qimen *gongfu*) 祁門功夫

The English name of the finest Chinese red, keemun, is a corruption of a place called Qimen, and refers to the mountainous area around Qimen County in Anhui Province. Likou, Shanli, and Pingli in Qimen County are reputed to produce the best keemun tea. For most of the Qing dynasty, Qimen was known for a fine green tea similar to the modern Liuan green. Then in 1875 a Fujian

Keemun

tea merchant moved into the area and began fully oxidizing the local tea in the style of Fujian reds. Southern Anhui turned out to have the ideal climate for fully oxidized tea, and its excellent reds fetched high prices. This new processing method caught on quickly. The production method for keemun is like that of other reds, except that oxidation takes place inside a room heated by a low fire.

Keemun is actually quite varied. Within the Qimen region, eight kinds of hybrid trees are grown, and all of the harvest is marketed under the name keemun. So-called mulberry leaf (*chuye*) tea makes up about 70% of output, and willow leaf (*liuye*) trees provide another 16%. The remaining 14% of production is divided among six other hybrids. Because the mulberry leaf tea tree is most common, its flavor is usually associated with keemun, but each hybrid yields tea with slightly different characteristics.

The area around Qimen is crisscrossed with rivers and streams that contain numerous small islands, mudflats, and sandbars, many of which have been planted with tea trees. In springtime and after heavy rains, low-lying tea farms are temporarily flooded, replenishing the topsoil with a fresh layer of rich silt. This natural fertilizer gives riverside tea an extraordinarily rich flavor. Although "sandbar tea" (*zhoucha*) is highly prized, it accounts for only about 10–15% of total keemun output.

Keemun leaves are popularly called "precious rays" because they taper sharply at the tip and their jet black hue is interrupted with streaks of gray. One sprout and two or three young leaves are harvested from each twig, and many leaves are covered with fine down. These young leaves are quite small and continue to shrink when dried, so premium keemun is easily distinguished by its unusually small leaves. About 90% of keemun tea is currently exported, and it often ends up blended with red tea from India or Sri Lanka and marketed under generic labels such as "English Breakfast" tea.

The finest keemun is always sold under its own name. Even so, keemun varies enormously in quality, and not all of it is good. Anyone tasting low grade keemun will rightly wonder what all the fuss is about, as it is tainted by a horrific sour flavor. Premium keemun is entirely different. The best leaves yield a rich red liquid with an intensely sweet and fragrant aroma and pure gentle flavor. Common scents include fruit, rose, orchid, and chocolate. The very finest keemun is so smooth that it can be brewed to the highest possible intensity without the slightest trace of bitterness. This tea is the ideal accompaniment to good chocolate.

Yunnan Red (*Dianhong gongfu*) 滇紅工夫

Yunnan red teas date back only to the 1930s. In the early twentieth century exports from India and Ceylon (now Sri Lanka) exploded, challenging Chinese supremacy in the international tea market. Processors in Yunnan responded by creating imitations of rival Indian teas. Initial production was small, but Yunnan reds gained a foothold in the international market and production steadily increased from the 1950s onward. Today about 20% of Yunnan tea production consists of red teas not intended for ageing.

Yunnan Red

Most Yunnan red tea is grown in the southern and western parts of the province. The leaves often come from large old feral trees similar to those that yield *puer* tea, although tea not intended for ageing is classified as big leaf *gongfu* instead of *puer*. The biological diversity of these semi-wild trees gives Yunnan reds a wide range of characteristics. Spring tea is best, while the summer and autumn flushes are less flavorful. The leaves are often covered with a fine yellow down, and the darker the color of this furry covering the later in the season the leaf was picked. The down on spring tea is light yellow, but by autumn it has turned dark gold. Also, leaves picked in summer tend to be much longer than those harvested in spring or autumn. Regardless of the harvest time, big leaf *gongfu* leaves are unusually large and thick. During processing they are crushed or tightly curled and oxidized until completely black.

The liquid is red and extremely fragrant with a rich caramel flavor. Although the finest Yunnan reds compare well with premium keemun, the taste is extremely complex and thus not nearly as smooth. If keemun is comparable to a gentle Darjeeling, Yunnan reds are closer to more assertive Assam brews. In fact, although keemun is more famous, many connoisseurs prefer the more complex taste of Yunnan reds. The liquid often carries wonderfully rich scents and flavors such as chocolate, *litchi*, banana, and brown sugar.

Ning Red (*Ninghong gongfu*) 寧紅工夫

This tea is produced in several counties in Jiangxi that include Xiushui, Wuning, and Tonggu. The region used to be called Ningzhou, hence the name Ning red. Although the area has produced tea since the Tang dynasty, Ning red dates to the late eighteenth century, making it one of the earliest red teas. Starting in the early nineteenth century, this tea was sold to Russian merchants who transported it by horse across Siberia to Europe, where it was sold as Russian caravan tea. Traditionally the best Ning red has been considered the equal of keemun, and the premium grade is excellent. The youngest of these black leaves are covered with fine golden fuzz. Some Ning red tea is tied into attractive bunches called dragon beards that weigh about a quarter ounce each.

Mass-Market Reds

Most Chinese red teas are mass produced for export and end up in generic blends. Even so, the higher grades of these workhorse teas are often worth drinking. Mass-market reds are usually classified very generally by province, and each has somewhat different characteristics, as noted below:

- **Yi Red (*Yihong gongfu*) 宜紅工夫**
  This tea is from the area around the Exishan area of Hubei, where it has been grown since about 1840 as an export commodity. Production was interrupted during the chaos of the 1920s and resumed in the 1950s. The leaves are dark, curled, and covered with golden down. The liquid is rich and thick with a sweet long-lasting fragrance.
- **Sichuan Red (*Chuanhong gongfu*) 川紅工夫**
  Produced in the southeastern portion of the province, this tea dates back only to the 1950s. The spring tea is most delicate, while leaves harvested later in the season have a heartier flavor. Mature leaves are fairly round, plump, and have some golden down. The sweet fragrant liquid is unusually dark and can be brewed until deep black.

- **Fujian Red (*Minhong gongfu*) 閩紅工夫**
This tea has been produced for export since the mid-nineteenth century. There are three main types—Zhenghe, Danyang, and Bailin—varying considerably in quality and taste. Zhenghe red is from northern Fujian, mostly the area around Zhenghe County, and is subdivided into big-leaf and small-leaf tea. Big-leaf Zhenghe red is better, with a rich sweet flavor, while the small-leaf variety is pleasant but weak. Danyang red was originally produced around Danyang Village near Mount Baiyun, although today it is grown in a wide area around Fuan. The thin sweet-smelling black leaves are covered with white down. Bailin red is named after the town of Bailin, where the tea grown around Mount Tailao in Fuding County is usually processed. The leaves are yellowish black, tightly curled, and covered with orange down. Their liquid is said to be the color of kumquats.

- **Hunan Red (*Huhong gongfu*) 湖紅工夫**
This tea comes from a wide swath of Hunan Province spreading out around Anhua County. Western tea merchants began buying Hunan tea in 1843, and by 1858 the local farmers were producing red tea specifically for export. Hunan farmers grow many hybrids, including some unusual heirloom varieties, so Hunan reds are extremely diverse and range in taste from slightly bitter to extremely smooth. The best Hunan tea, such as that from Anhua, has plump and tightly curled leaves, and the deep red liquid is richly aromatic. Other Hunan reds have a much lighter taste.

- **Zhejiang Red (*Yuehong gongfu*) 越紅工夫**
This tea, produced around Wenzhou in Zhejiang Province, saw large-scale production begin in the 1950s. The black leaves are relatively uniform, straight, and tightly curled, and the downy sprouts are silver or gray. The liquid is a relatively light shade of red or orange. Most Zhejiang red is fairly weak, although tea grown around the Pu River tends to brew a darker, heavier beverage.

Sun Moon Red (Riyue *hong*) 日月紅

Most of Taiwan's red tea is grown on the mountains around picturesque Sun Moon Lake in Nantou County. In 1935, when Taiwan was still a Japanese colony, middlemen imported trees from India with the intention of creating an imitation Indian tea for the international market. This tea's sub-continental origins make it unique among Chinese reds. Outside of Yunnan, Chinese red tea comes from small-leaf native trees, whereas the most famous Taiwanese red is made from big-leaf Indian-style hybrids, giving it a flavor reminiscent of good Assam tea. Some farmers in the area also produce tea from small-leaf native trees that tastes surprisingly similar to the trademark tea from Indian plants.

Taiwanese red tea was exported in large quantities during the mid-twentieth century and often ended up in tea bags or generic blends. At the height of production, more than 1,700 tons were exported every year. However, as labor costs rose, Taiwanese farmers could no longer compete with red tea from low wage countries. Today not even 200 tons of this tea is produced every year, and less is produced every season. From a high-volume export tea, Sun Moon red is being rebranded as a premium specialty item.

Stiff international competition has forced Taiwan's red tea producers to be especially creative. They were disappointed to find imported tea trees inadequate by local standards, so Japanese and Taiwanese agronomists spent decades developing improved hybrids. Some tea is still produced from the original unimproved Indian trees and marketed under the name Assam red. The flavor of this heirloom tea is fairly insipid, and it is obvious why Taiwanese experts thought that it needed improvement. Their labors have resulted in two far superior varieties. Taiwan red No. 8 is the lighter, No. 18 the heavier of the two. Some farmers around Sun Moon Lake have also begun using these hybrids to grow organic tea.

Big-leaf Sun Moon red stands out because of its unusually large leaves, although the small-leaf variety resembles reds from mainland China. After brewing, the brown damp leaves of the big leaf variety often appear mottled with green patches where the leaf is less oxidized. These green areas give this tea more complexity than most red teas. Sun Moon red is extremely similar in taste to Oriental beauty, the most heavily oxidized Taiwanese oolong, although it is not nearly as acrid. Whether big leaf or small, the flavor of Sun Moon red is pleasantly bitter on the tongue and balanced with a sweet throat, much like Assam's very best tea.

Lapsang souchong (**Zhengshan** *xiaozhong*) 正山小種

This peculiar tea is produced in Fujian around the famed Mount Wuyi. Although the area yields decent red tea, the geography and climate are better suited to oolong. Fully oxidized tea is rarely grown near Mount Wuyi with the exception of a small amount of smoked red tea. By 1604 a kind of tea called *xiaozhong* (small variety) was being produced there. It is unclear what the original tea of this name was like, and it probably was not smoked. The term now refers to the smoked red teas produced around Wuyi.

The Chinese name Zhengshan *xiaozhong* refers to a local mountain (Zhengshan) and the variety of tea (*xiaozhong*). In English, this has been bastardized into *lapsang souchong*. Chinese usually refer to it more directly as smoked tea. No one knows when smoked tea was first produced. There are legends regarding its origins, but none is reliable. Huge amounts of tea from the area were exported during the late nineteenth century, and shipments probably included a small amount of the local smoked tea, giving it a toehold in the international market.

Lapsang souchong is made from relatively mature leaves, two or three per twig. The production process is unique. First, the leaves are put in a long wooden building specially designed to allow smoke to circulate freely. Inside, smoldering pinewood fires produce heat that gently withers the leaves as they absorb the fumes. The leaves are turned a few times to expose them evenly to the heat and smoke. This step lasts for about 90 minutes. Next, the leaves are put outside to air and to continue drying. They are then rolled to twist them and are allowed to oxidize in a warm place for 5–6 hours. Oxidization is stopped by tossing the leaves into a hot wok, after which they are rolled again and smoked over a low pinewood fire to finish drying and intensify the flavor. This peculiar processing method turns the leaves jet black, and they brew a dark murky liquid that exudes a strong smoky smell. *Lapsang souchong* is exceptionally complex, acrid, and oily. It tastes strongly of smoke, cinnamon, chestnuts, and fruit in addition to far more challenging flavors.

Smoked tea is definitely an acquired taste. Most Chinese recoil in horror from this brew, which is extremely harsh, and nowadays it is mainly produced for export. Despite the unenthusiastic reception in its homeland, *lapsang souchong* has managed to find a niche in the West where some people consider it sophisticated. It has even been immortalized on film as James Bond's preferred tea. Smoked tea makes an interesting chaser or mixer for whisky, and this striking cocktail is guaranteed to elicit some interesting reactions from startled guests. I recommend mixing it with Laphroaig scotch.

Chapter 10

Black Tea

Tea leaves are sometimes stored under special conditions to encourage the growth of microbes, a mysterious process that changes tea in unpredictable ways. Chinese have deliberately aged tea since at least the eleventh century. When done properly, this technique not only enriches flavor and aroma but also makes each batch of leaves unique. Ageing is completely different from oxidation, when enzyme molecules in the moist leaf bond with oxygen. In contrast, the growth of foreign organisms on the leaf during ageing is akin to the fermentation that creates wine, bread, and yogurt.

Ageing can endow a tea with intense complexity and singular personality. Old characteristics disappear while new ones emerge, so some good qualities are usually sacrificed for the sake of others. Aged teas often have very odd tastes and smells, making them an acquired taste—these are the tea world's single malt scotches. Their fans consider aged teas the finest of all brews, although many informed drinkers do not care for them. A tea can be coaxed in many different directions during ageing, leaving enormous room for creativity and serendipity. This endless potential makes aged tea a particularly fascinating niche in the Chinese tea world. In addition to the diverse range of unusual flavors, ageing is also reputed to impart medicinal qualities to the leaves.

Many connoisseurs age tea at home for their own consumption. A few ambitious drinkers even set some tea aside to be consumed by their children and grandchildren. Tea leaves aged since a child's birth make an impressive thirtieth birthday present, and wedding anniversaries can be celebrated in style with tea harvested during the year of marriage. Some teashop owners and farmers also age tea that they sell decades later at very high prices. Although few varieties of aged tea can be found sitting on the teahouse shelf, a well-connected merchant can help you locate tea of a specific kind or year, although you can expect to pay handsomely for this service.

Tea can be put down in many different ways, and each variety reacts differently to specific conditions. This makes ageing tea a tricky business. If done incorrectly, the leaves might develop a disgusting rotten flavor or else become stale and tasteless. When successful, however, the results can be intriguing. Tea leaves shrink and darken over time and sometimes end up covered with a thin powder of mildew. Even so, in many good aged teas the smell of mildew is completely absent. Aged green tea can end up resembling good oolong, although with the addition of some unusual flavors. Well-aged oolong might become smooth, pleasant, and heavy, like a red tea only more complex. Alternatively, if aged in a different way, the same oolong can turn incredibly strong and assertive.

Red tea is by far the most common choice for ageing, and certain teashops specialize in this unusual product. After ageing, red tea is called black tea. This term has completely different meanings in English and Chinese. To Westerners, black tea refers to any fully oxidized tea like those from India and Sri Lanka, which Chinese would call red tea. Aged red tea, known to Chinese as black tea, is unlike anything regularly consumed in the West.

Puer 普洱

Puer tea (also known as *pu-erh*) from southern Yunnan is by far the most famous black tea. In imperial times *puer* was consumed mostly in the remote regions of south and west China and Tibet. Today the Cantonese are probably the greatest *puer* connoisseurs, even though the first shipment did not arrive in Hong Kong until 1941. This tea inspires cult-like fanaticism, and missionary work by small circles of *puer* zealots is steadily winning over converts.

The name *puer* is misleading, as this tea is not grown near the town of Puer. The leaves are actually harvested around Xishuangbanna in the Golden Triangle region near the border with Thailand and Burma, far to the south of the town of Puer. The name *puer* comes from the fact that the entire area was originally part of an administrative region called Puer, named after the district capital, which included all of southernmost Yunnan. Most of the area's native inhabitants are ethnic minorities, not Han Chinese, and their taste in tea has shaped the development of *puer*.

The definition of *puer* varies from person to person, and the term often refer generally to any teas like those produced around Xishuangbanna. According to one count, there are forty-two kinds of *puer* tea, thirty-one made in the Xishuangbanna area. Similar teas are also produced in northern Vietnam, northern Thailand, and elsewhere in China, including Guangdong, Sichuan, Henan, and Anhui. To make classic Yunnan *puer*, the leaves are fully oxidized into red tea, compressed into a solid mass (usually a hard disk), then aged to mellow out the flavor. Strictly speaking, *puer* is still red tea when young, and it should be considered black only after ageing, but most people refer to all *puer*, young and old, as black tea. Generally speaking, when it comes to *puer* the older the better. Although most *puer* is fully oxidized, green *puer* is also available. When aged, green *puer* combines the light vegetable taste of green leaves with the musty flavor of ageing. It is far less mellow than standard black *puer* and has a much smaller market.

Puer is produced near the original range of the wild tea tree, so its origins might well be quite ancient. Although Chinese records from the ninth century mention tea from southern Yunnan, Tang and Song dynasty tea-drinkers never included it in their accounts, so it does not seem to have been regularly consumed by ethnic Chinese. By the thirteenth century, tea exports from Yunnan were already significant, although it seems that most Chinese still looked down on Yunnan tea as an inferior product. At that time Yunnan was becoming more closely tied to China, and the number of Han Chinese living there grew steadily. As more Chinese came into direct contact with Yunnan tea, exports increased and this exotic beverage became more widely known. By the early Qing dynasty, Chinese were referring to tea from southern Yunnan as *puer*.

Puer came of age when the Qing dynasty court designated it an official article of tribute. The ancestors of that dynasty's emperors were Manchu nomads before they conquered China, so they consumed unusually large quantities of meat. The Manchus apparently took to *puer* because of its renowned digestive properties and drank it regularly during winter. *Puer* was first designated a tribute tea in 1729, and afterwards it was received annually at court until 1908. Once the emperors began drinking *puer* it instantly acquired cachet. Producing tea for the demanding palates of the imperial court also undoubtedly spurred *puer* farmers and processors to create a more sophisticated product.

No one knows when ageing became a regular part of *puer* production. Tea used to be exported from Yunnan by caravan, and some authorities suspect that the long journey to distant markets gave the tea enough time to ferment. Consumers may have acquired a taste for this inadvertently aged tea and began to demand it. A new process initiated in 1973 simulates ageing by storing the leaves briefly in a hot humid room, giving them a quick round of forced fermentation prior to sale.

Puer Qizi *Disks, Wrapped and Unwrapped*

Puer *Tea Bricks, Wrapped and Unwrapped*

Puer produced by this method is called mature (*shou*) tea. In contrast, tea that leaves the factory without undergoing speedy pseudo-ageing is referred to as raw (*sheng*) tea. This jargon is misleading, however, because so-called mature tea is still far from its peak and deserves further ageing. Nevertheless, the distinction is still useful because raw and mature leaves have distinctive characteristics and react differently to ageing. Large government-owned factories produce tea according to fairly uniform methods, and all of their output can be classified as mature. Newer private tea processors have more leeway to experiment with new techniques, and raw disks come from these smaller tea companies.

The easiest way to determine whether *puer* is mature or raw is to ask the person selling it. If the proprietor does not know the difference, you should probably buy your tea elsewhere. On your own there are several ways to tell the difference. First, you can look at the brand. Tea put out by a large state-owned factory (such as the famous *qizi* disks) is definitely mature, whereas a boutique brand might be either mature or raw. State-owned tea companies usually have long communist-sounding names (such as China National Native Produce and Animal By-Products Import and Export Corporation, Yunnan Tea Branch), while the names of private brands are more concise. Physical details also provide useful clues. A raw disk often has a slick surface, and the leaves are sometimes (but not always) still slightly green. This tea brews a reddish liquid with a lighter taste, and when young the flavor often resembles green tea. The leaves of mature tea are always quite dark, and parts of individual leaves stand out somewhat from the surface so the disk feels slightly bumpy. Mature tea usually yields a strong-tasting black liquid. Some drinkers complain that the flavor is strangely artificial and tastes unpleasantly of mildew, although others relish the intensity. Even after ageing, mature tea maintains a hearty flavor, whereas raw tea can still be fairly delicate after twenty years or more.

Puer is sometimes aged for many decades. When the Qing dynasty fell, the remaining stock of imperial tea came into the hands of the Chinese government. In 1963, more than two tons of imperial tribute tea remained, some of it more than 150 years old. Unfortunately, that year China faced a tea shortage, so the Communist government ground up the priceless imperial *puer*, mixed it with inferior grades, and sold it anonymously in ordinary blends. Chinese connoisseurs still weep at the thought of this atrocity.

Puer comes from a unique variety of tree known to science as *Camellia assamica* [*Masters*] *Chang*, which Chinese tea-drinkers refer to much more concisely as big-leaf tea. These plants are genetically close to wild tea. Because they are so well-suited to the Yunnan climate, big-leaf trees are allowed to grow in an almost feral state and reach several yards in height. After planting, the trees are usually not actively tended, so within a few years the untrained eye can hardly distinguish a tea plantation from the surrounding forest. Some of these semi-wild plantations are very old, and their tea is considered extremely desirable. Unfortunately, many ancient plantations were cut down during the 1960s and 1970s to make room for higher-yielding modern varieties that connoisseurs regard as inferior.

Some of the methods used to produce *puer* are almost identical to the way tea was made in the Tang and Song dynasties. First, the leaves are stirred in a large hot wok, then crinkled and left to oxidize for a time. Afterwards they are crinkled and oxidized again. The leaves are then exposed to the sun until 40–50% dry. Next, they are crumpled again and then baked until fully dry. Then the dry leaves are steamed until soft then put into small cloth bags and crumpled by hand. A cloth bag full of moist leaves is placed inside a mold and a weight is put on top. The leaves stay in the mold until fully dry, at which point they have been compressed into a hard mass, usually a disk or brick shape. Mature tea is then put in a humid room to undergo a rapid fermentation similar to ageing while raw tea is sold immediately as is.

Most *puer* tea is drunk soon after purchase, but ambitious drinkers buy disks with the intention of ageing them further. Tea disks aged in private hands are referred to as "collected," and if done properly, the tea increases in both taste and monetary value. Because of their value, the most expensive specimens are bought and sold, lovingly examined, caressed, discussed, argued over, and set aside for yet more ageing, but rarely consumed. Hong Kong is the center of *puer* appreciation, and local teahouses age enormous quantities of *puer* in special storerooms. Each teahouse ages their tea somewhat differently, thereby lending it a distinctive flavor. Some people patronize a particular teahouse just because they like the black tea, so ageing methods are often closely guarded commercial secrets. To the untrained eye, some of the leaves in these storerooms appear to be in appalling condition. The leaves often develop a noble rot called "white frost," are nibbled at by rats and insects, and look little different from piles of garbage. All that matters, however, is the final flavor, and this can become spectacular if the tea is aged properly.

Enthusiasts also age tea at home, and bedrooms and offices sometimes have a "tea mountain" of old disks stacked in a corner. Anyone intending to age tea should proceed with care. If you do not do this correctly, the tea will be completely ruined. *Puer* fans like to swap hair-raising tales of expensive tea that was spoiled through improper ageing. There are no hard-and-fast rules for ageing, which is more an art than a science. Tea can be aged in many different ways, and each method brings out a slightly different flavor in the leaves. Different wild microbes float through the air in each place, and each kind of bacteria or fungus acts on the leaves in a special way, so no two aged teas are ever exactly the same. Trial and error are an inevitable part of the process, but over time you might discover a home ageing method that produces excellent tea.

The first step is to make sure that the tea is worth putting down. An informed *puer* dealer can tell you which varieties age well, as some improve far more than others. Also, the final taste will vary considerably depending upon the type of tea being aged (such as raw vs. mature), so you should choose a variety that is likely to end up as something you will enjoy. Next, it is vital to select the proper location. Tea should always be stored away from sunlight and apart from foods and other items that might taint its flavor. The tea needs to be somewhere with good ventilation lest it develop harmful molds and mildew. Light is always destructive to tea, so if it is not being kept in a dark room, store your *puer* in paper bags to block out all light. Unlike ordinary tea, leaves being aged should not be kept in airtight containers, as this will prevent microbial growth. When buying tea to age, it is best to buy a stack of seven or so disks wrapped in dried bamboo leaves, as *puer* kept inside the original packaging will probably age best. You can also have fun watching your perplexed friends as they try to guess the contents of the odd leaf-wrapped bundle that has been sitting on your bookshelf for the past ten years.

Temperature and humidity are the most important factors influencing how tea ages. Generally speaking, the higher the temperature the faster tea ferments, but if the leaves become too hot or too cold, the microbes die and fermentation stops. Also, if the air is not humid enough, there will not be enough moisture for microbes to grow, and the leaves will become desiccated and lifeless. On the other hand, if the air is too moist, the tea might rot. The ideal storage climate fluctuates between 20°–35° C (70°–95° F) with humidity between 70–85%. These conditions are easily found in wet subtropical Hong Kong, but they might be harder to achieve elsewhere. In that case, you have no choice but to pay a top price for tea that has already been properly aged in an appropriate location.

During ageing, the characteristics of the leaves slowly alter under the action of various microscopic organisms. Although tea leaves teeming with microbes might not sound appealing, these creatures are less fearsome than they sound. Common ageing agents include the fungi *Aspergillus niger*, *Aspergillus glaucus*, and *Rhizopus* as well as bacteria such as *Lactobacillus thermophilus* (also found in yogurt), molds such as *Penicillium* (the famous antibiotic), and wild yeast (the organism that makes bread rise). The proportion of each ageing agent varies considerably in each place, giving every batch of old tea unique qualities.

Several problems can occur during ageing. You should occasionally sniff the tea to make sure all is going well. If a disk feels soft, it has absorbed too much water. In that case just unwrap it and allow it to sit in a warm dry place for a few days to dry out. It might also be necessary to buy a dehumidifier for the storage area. If the tea is so dry that it becomes brittle, put it somewhere more humid. Mildew comes in many forms. A light dusting of white mildew is usually no problem and even adds to a tea's flavor, but you have to use commonsense to decide whether you like what a particular fungus is doing to your tea. Round spots of mold are always undesirable. A moldy or excessively mildewed disk can sometimes be salvaged by unwrapping it and scrubbing the surface with a clean, dry, new toothbrush. Tea disks and packaging occasionally become infested with insects such as silverfish or small moth caterpillars, but you can still usually save the tea by carefully removing any insects and scrubbing the surface with a dry toothbrush.

Probably the most difficult part of ageing is simply to forget about the tea and not drink it. *Puer* generally takes twenty years to reach its peak under optimal ageing conditions, although the timeframe varies widely depending upon the tea and the environment. Hong Kong tea-drinkers like to muse about semi-mythical "forgotten tea." According to local legend, some teahouses store so much old tea that they lose track of their stock, occasionally discovering dusty tea disks in an obscure nook of the storeroom that have been sitting there for many decades. These serendipitous mistakes allow the proprietor's friends to enjoy some of the finest *puer* available anywhere.

For those too impatient to age tea themselves, or fortunate enough not to live someplace as hot and humid as Hong Kong, old tea is available for sale. However, buyers who intend to pay large sums for very old *puer* should be cautious. Old *puer* has become so expensive that counterfeiting is a major problem. Moreover, unlike wine, the production date rarely appears on *puer* disks, so it is difficult to determine the exact age. Although a few private factories have started printing the harvest date on the wrapper, this sensible practice is still uncommon. Some fanatical collectors study minute changes in packaging to try to determine the age of their disks, and there are fantastically detailed articles and books in Chinese dedicated to this arcane pursuit. It is impossible for the average person to date a disk with precision, although with experience you can distinguish newer from older tea by the odor of the leaves. To avoid being cheated, anyone planning to invest in high grade aged *puer* should buy from an informed and reputable dealer. Even so, you are still taking a chance because most old tea has probably changed hands several times.

During the hysteria leading up to the return of Hong Kong to China in 1997, some teahouses and collectors sold off their prize *puer*, bringing some of the finest rare old tea onto the open market. However, there is no good reason to make a fetish out of age or price. Some types of *puer* start off much better than others, and even lengthy ageing cannot make up the difference. I have tasted excellent 7-year-old *puer* that was preferable to mediocre 35-year-old tea. Good *puer* is not necessarily very old, nor is old tea always good, and a relatively economical tea is often as tasty as something much pricier. Also, in the last few years a new type of *puer* has come out that is designed to peak in flavor while relatively young, and this convenient new style seems to herald the future for black tea.

Sometimes *puer* is sold in loose-leaf form or else the compressed tea cake is torn apart into individual leaves prior to sale. Usually, though, *puer* is compressed into several standard shapes. Disks are most common, and these come in a perplexing array of brands and grades. *Puer* is also compressed into bricks and also an odd shape called a *tuo*, a hemisphere with either a hollow interior or stem that can look rather like a huge mushroom. The term *qizi* (also spelled *chi tse*) refers to superior *puer* disks produced for export, and many of the disks purchased outside of China carry this designation.

Since 1973 it has been common for large state-owned factories to identify disks with a four-digit code such as 7532 or 8582. The first two digits refer to the year when this sort of tea was first produced. The third digit records the type of manufacturing process used, and the fourth reveals the identity of the factory that processed the tea. For example, tea number 7532 was first produced in 1975 and was made according to manufacturing process number three by Factory No. 2. While most drinkers will not find this information immediately useful, the number serves as a kind of brand that can help you keep track of the many different types of disks, each of which has a distinctive flavor.

Before brewing *puer* you have to hack off a chunk of tea from the disk. Because the leaves have been tightly compressed, this is easier said than done. Never use a knife or fork, as these can easily slip and cause injury. Special tools for separating off a hunk of leaves are available at teashops, although a short flat-edged screwdriver works equally well. The compressed leaves tend to settle in layers, so the trick is to insert the blade between two layers of leaves so that you can easily pry off a piece. If you are impatient, you can just wrap the disk in newspaper and smash it up with a hammer.

As with other oxidized teas, the water for brewing old *puer* should be on the hot side, near 100° C (215° F). If the tea is still young and slightly green, however, the water ought to be somewhat cooler. *Puer* can be brewed in a small pot, although black tea is so hearty that it can stand up to a large pot too. If brewed in a small pot, decent *puer* leaves are good for eight to ten infusions. In the average Cantonese restaurant a large pot of tea sits on the table throughout the meal, and waiters continuously add water to the same leaves. In expensive Hong Kong restaurants, high quality aged *puer* is sometimes carefully brewed to perfection in the kitchen and brought out in a large serving pot without leaves, ensuring that the tea is always at optimum strength. Although black tea has an assertive taste, good restaurants often brew it fairly weak to lend it the delicacy appropriate for an accompaniment to fine food.

Puer leaves vary considerably in color, shape, and size, though they are usually much larger than ordinary Chinese tea leaves. Aged *puer* often has a musty odor that seems unpromising on first encounter, although its fans enjoy the challenging complexity. This tea can be brewed to impressive intensity and will take on a terrifying shade of inky black if allowed to steep for a long time. Even so, good *puer* is extremely mellow. The tea carries a hint of sweetness balanced with a slight pleasant bitterness and enriched by the heavy woody flavor of ageing. The remarkable contrast of strength and mellowness stands out as the hallmark of fine *puer*. Enthusiasts prize this mellowness and refer to it by the Zen-like expression "the tasteless taste" or "the flavor of no flavor." *Puer* tea is the perfect accompaniment for heavy meat dishes and oily foods.

Liubao 六堡

Black tea from Guangxi is usually marketed as Liubao. This name is taken from Liubao District in Cangwu County, although this tea is, in fact, produced over a large area covering more than two dozen counties in Guangxi. Black tea has been made in Guangxi for the past two centuries and comes from the same sort of big-leaf old trees used to make *puer*, so the qualities and flavors of the two teas are similar. Liubao black tea is produced in both loose-leaf and compressed forms. The compressed tea is either shaped into disks, like classic *puer*, or else packed into dried bamboo leaves that are twisted into a long tube and tied off in four places to form a series of five bulbs.

A sprout and two to four leaves are harvested from each stem. These are heated over a fire, crinkled, oxidized, crinkled again, and then dried. Ageing turns the leaves dark brown or black. They yield a rich red liquid with a hint of sweetness, a subtle citrus flavor, and a delicate taste compared to betel nut. Ageing also imparts a strong smoky aroma and sometimes a slight undertaste of mildew. Tea packed in bamboo leaves gradually absorbs some of the bamboo scent as it ages. The people of Guangxi believe that old Liubao tea has medicinal value.

Liuan Black Tea (Liuan *heicha*) 六安黑茶

A black tea named after Liuan County in Anhui Province makes a less expensive alternative to aged Yunnan *puer*, although it is usually not as tasty. In the tea world the term Liuan can refer to any tea produced in the general area around Liuan County, and most of this tea does not come from Liuan itself. This area is most famous for yellow and green teas, although some red tea is also made specifically for ageing into black tea. Black Liuan is usually packed into baskets with a broad open top. This is covered over with dried leaves, and the tea is left to age. It is usually removed from the basket prior to sale and marketed in loose-leaf form. The leaves are curled and highly irregular in shape and size; after ageing they range in color from crimson to dark brown. Aged Liuan usually has a heavy mildewed odor, so it is a good idea to wash the leaves with a quick flush of hot water to eliminate any unpleasant residues. After brewing, however, the rich orange liquid exudes only the slightest fragrance. The taste is mellow and slightly sweet with some woody flavor from ageing.

Hunan Black Tea (Hunan *heicha*) 湖南黑茶

Black tea was being manufactured in Hunan during the sixteenth century, apparently in imitation of aged teas from Sichuan. Hunan black tea was originally produced in the area bordering the Zi River, but today it comes from a large region that stretches across Hunan. This tea has become more popular in recent years, and a large amount is now produced.

Unlike *puer*, black tea from Hunan is usually loose-leaf. During processing the leaves are heated over a fire, crinkled, oxidized, rolled, then heated again until completely dry. Finally, the leaves are sorted into four grades and aged for a time before sale. Top quality leaves are a uniform shade of black, tender, tightly curled, and produce an orange liquid. The flavor of top grade Hunan black tea is rich and smoky yet not at all acrid.

Old Green Tea (*lao qingcha*) 老青茶

Aged Hunan green tea, called simply "old green tea" (*lao qingcha*), dates back to at least the nineteenth century. Unlike most green teas, it is compressed into a brick and then aged to give more complexity. The leaves are picked at various times of year and classed into two grades. Finer leaves become *miancha*, the premium variety. These are stirred over a fire, crinkled, sun dried, heated again, and set out in the sun once more until completely dry. The inferior grade (*licha*) is made from coarser leaves. The finest *miancha* has tightly curled dark green leaves and white stems. Lesser grades are marked by red stems and yellowed leaves.

Sichuan Border Tea (Sichuan *biancha*) 四川邊茶

This tea is descended from compressed teas produced in Sichuan during the Song dynasty. Sichuan black tea was mostly exported to peoples living to the west. During the Qing dynasty, black tea from the region was divided into two types. Southern border tea was exported to Tibet, while western border tea was sold in the remote mountainous western regions of Sichuan. Each is produced in areas around the trade routes leading to their respective markets. Sichuan border tea has never been considered fine tea, and Chinese traditionally looked down on it as rubbish to be pawned off on ignorant foreigners.

Southern border tea is made from old coarse leaves mixed with numerous stems. These are processed in various ways and come in many grades. The leaves are steamed and usually compressed into bricks during processing. Western border tea is even coarser and is often made from leathery mature leaves that are one or two years old at harvest. Each brick consists of 20–60% of stems. The use of thick old leaves and a phenomenal number of stems gives border tea an extremely harsh flavor that most people find unappealing.

Aged Cliff Tea (*lao yancha*) 老岩茶

During the Song dynasty heyday of teas from Mount Wuyi in Fujian, the local tea was routinely compressed into disks and other shapes. However, with the rise of loose-leaf tea, Fujian tea disks gradually fell out of favor and disappeared. In the last few years this custom has been unexpectedly revived. The popularity (and high prices) of fine *puer* have inspired some producers in northern Fujian to compress fine oolong cliff tea into disks and bricks intended for ageing. The long-term development of this tea has yet to be seen, although the taste of compressed cliff tea already seems extremely promising after just a few years. The flavor is like ordinary cliff tea, but with added complexity and mellowness from the ageing process.

Appendices

Glossary of Specialized Terms

baihao 白毫
cha 茶
chajing 茶經
chen 陳
dacha 大茶
dan 淡
gan 甘 (sweet), 乾 (dry)
gongfu 功夫
houlong 喉嚨
huo 活
ku 苦
nong 濃
qi 氣 (lively), 旗 (banner)

qiang 槍
qing 青
qizi 七子
se 澀
sheng 生
shou 熟
shunkou 順口
suan 酸
tu 茶
tuo 沱
xiaocha 小茶
zisha 紫沙

Glossary of Tea Names

Alishan *wulong* 阿里山烏龍
Anxi *sezhong* 安溪色種
Anxi *tie Guanyin* 安溪鐵觀音
baihao wulong 白毫烏龍
Baihe *longjing* 白鶴龍井
Bailin *gongfu* 白琳工夫
bai mudan 白牡丹
Bajiaoting *longxu* 八角亭龍須
baozhong 包種
Beigang *maojian* 北港毛尖
benshan 本山
Chuan *hong gongfu* 川紅工夫
chuye 楮葉
cuiyu 翠玉
daye 大葉
Dayuling *wulong* 大禹嶺烏龍
Dian *hong gongfu* 滇紅工夫
dongding wulong 凍頂烏龍
dongfang meiren 東方美人
Dongting Biluo *chun* 洞庭碧螺春
Fenghuang *cha* 鳳凰茶
ganlu 甘露
gaoshan wulong 高山烏龍

gongfu 工夫
gongmei 貢眉
Guangdong *daye qing* 廣東大葉青
Guzhu *zisun* 顧渚紫笋
Haimagong *cha* 海馬宮茶
hongcha 紅茶
huanghua yunjian 黃花雲尖
huangjin gui 黃金桂
Huangshan *maofeng* 黃山毛峰
Hu *hong gongfu* 湖紅工夫
Hunan *heicha* 湖南黑茶
Huoshan *huangya* 霍山黃芽
Hupao *longjing* 虎跑龍井
Huzhou *zisun* 湖州紫笋
jian cha 尖茶
Jing *xian tejian* 涇縣特尖
jinhuang pian 金黃片
jinxuan 金萱
jiuqu hongmei 九曲紅梅
Junshan *yinzhen* 君山銀針
lao qingcha 老青茶
lao yancha 老岩茶
licha 里茶

Lishan *wulong* 梨山烏龍
Liuan 六安
Liuan *heicha* 六安黑茶
Liuan *guapian* 六安瓜片
Liubao 六堡
liuye 柳葉
longjing 龍井
lü mudan 綠牡丹
Luyuan *maojian* 鹿苑毛尖
maoxie 毛蟹
maozhen 毛針
Meijiawu *longjing* 梅家塢龍井
meizhan 梅占
Mengding *huangya* 蒙頂黃芽
miancha 面茶
Minbei *shuixian* 閩北水仙
Min *hong gongfu* 閩紅工夫
Muzha *tie Guanyin* 木柵鐵觀音
Nangang *baozhong* 南港包種
Ning *hong gongfu* 寧紅工夫
Pingdong *gangkou cha* 屏東港口茶
Pingshui *zhucha* 平水珠茶
puer 普洱
qilan 奇蘭
Qimen *gongfu* 祁門功夫
Qishan *mingpian* 齊山名片
Riyue *hong* 日月紅
sezhong wulong 色種烏龍
Shanlinxi *wulong* 杉林溪烏龍
Shifeng *longjing* 獅峰龍井

shihua 石花
shoumei 壽眉
Sichuan *biancha* 四川邊茶
siji chun 四季春
Taiping *houkui* 太平猴魁
Tanyang *gongfu* 坦洋工夫
Tianzhu *longjing* 天竺龍井
Wanxi *huang dacha* 皖西黃大茶
Weishan *baimaojian* 溈山白毛尖
Wenshan *baozhong* 文山包種
Wenzhou *huangtang* 溫州黃湯
wulong 烏龍
Wuyi *bai jiguan* 武夷白雞冠
Wuyi *da hongpao* 武夷大紅袍
Wuyi *shui jingui* 武夷水金龜
Wuyi *tie luohan* 武夷鐵羅漢
Wuyi *rougui* 武夷肉桂
Wuyi *yancha* 武夷岩茶
xiangya se 象牙色
xiaobai 小白
xiaoye 小葉
xiaozhong 小種
Yi *hong gongfu* 宜紅工夫
yinzhen baihao 銀針白毫
Yongchun *foshou* 永春佛手
Yue *hong gongfu* 越紅工夫
Yunqi *longjing* 雲栖龍井
Zhenghe *gongfu* 政和工夫
Zhengshan *xiaozhong* 正山小種
zhoucha 洲茶

Index

Index

Index